W9-ABV-035

THE ULTIMATE GUIDE TO
WEATHER

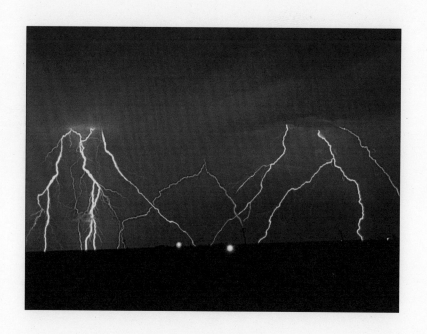

THE ULTIMATE GUIDE TO
WEATHER

JULIE LLOYD

EDITED BY JANE BENN AND DUNCAN JOHN

Bath · New York · Singapore · Hong Kong · Cologne · Delhi
Melbourne · Amsterdam · Johannesburg · Auckland · Shenzhen

This edition published by Parragon in 2011

Parragon
Queen Street House
4 Queen Street
Bath, BA1 1HE, UK
www.parragon.com

Produced by Atlantic Publishing

See page 256 for
photograph copyright details
Text © Parragon Books Ltd 2007

All rights reserved.
No part of this publication
may be reproduced or transmitted
in any form or by any means,
electronic or mechanical,
including photocopying,
recording, or any information storage
and retrieval system, without
permission in writing
from the copyright holders.

ISBN 978-1-4454-5396-5
Printed in China

CONTENTS

Contents

The Atmosphere: Local Patterns 82

Weather Extremes 104

Unusual Weather Opticals 142

History and Culture 154

Contents

Modern Weather Forecasting 170

Harnessing the Weather 188

Past Climates 198

Future Climates 210

Weather Records 242

INTRODUCTION

For many of us the weather is only of interest when it comes to deciding each morning what to wear, or perhaps when considering where to take a holiday. Is it cold or hot? Will it rain or be windy? At other times it becomes an issue only when there is something unusual taking place, such as a period of extreme heat or a storm.

However, increasingly, we have become interested in the weather as we read about and experience more unusual effects. Media coverage is extensive and often inaccurately scaremongering. This comprehensive book covers all areas of the weather, from how clouds are formed to explanations of the more extreme weather conditions as well as some of the optical events associated with the weather. Modern methods of weather forecasting are explained, methods of changing the weather discussed, and predictions about future weather problems analyzed. Understanding the weather, tracing its causes and effects, can only enhance our understanding of the Earth and Nature, and help us to live in harmony with both.

WEATHER
AND CLIMATES

WEATHER

Meteorology, the scientific study of the weather, has developed significantly during the last 50 years but we have reliable records for at least two centuries. There is a significant body of supplementary information, however, from a variety of historical sources which is now being explored to enable us to have a much clearer picture of the past. This might help us to better understand not only the past but also predict the future.

The Earth's atmosphere is constantly in motion and it is this which creates our weather. Weather is usually defined as the current state of the atmosphere in a place and time. The weather is, arguably, generally regarded as being of a relatively small scale both in terms of area and time. Weather forecasts are prepared frequently, on at least a daily basis, for a given location. In contrast, climate is seen as the longer term general state of the atmosphere—the typical weather for a location. It takes into consideration long-term averages, usually over a minimum of 30 years. This is designed to eliminate the effects of "freak" events and so give a clearer picture of what to expect.

CLIMATE

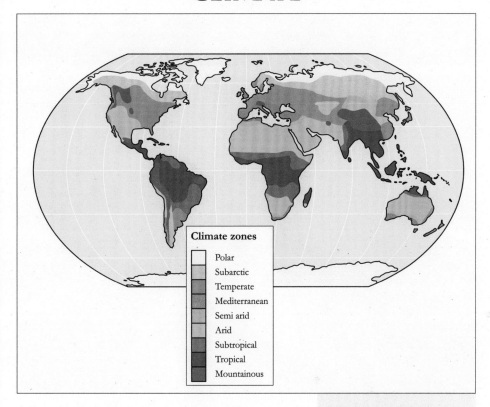

Climate zones
- Polar
- Subarctic
- Temperate
- Mediterranean
- Semi arid
- Arid
- Subtropical
- Tropical
- Mountainous

The average weather conditions of a place are called its climate. The most important conditions are the average monthly temperatures and average monthly rainfall. The world is divided into regions according to their climate, although the boundaries are not sharply defined, as one type of climate gradually merges into the next. In addition, every year is different; for example, the occasional long hot summers over north-west Europe are called Mediterranean type summers because they more closely reflect that climate. In broad terms, climate zones range in latitude from tropical (hot; no real seasons based on temperature) to mid-latitude (moderate; conventional winter-spring-summer-fall seasons) to polar (cold; strong seasonality; long winters).

The first person to define the climatic zones was the Greek philosopher Aristotle (384–322 BC). He divided the world into three zones (torrid, temperate, and frigid) based on the height of the sun above the horizon. Modern climatic maps show many more regions using a variety of criteria including latitude, height above sea level, distance from the ocean, temperature, and precipitation.

TROPICAL CLIMATES

The rainforest is divided into four distinct parts. The emergent layer contains the small number of trees which grow above the general canopy. The canopy contains the majority of the larger trees; it is estimated that it is home to 40 percent of all plant species. The understory layer is the space between the canopy and the forest floor and is home to numerous birds, snakes and lizards. The forest floor is relatively clear of vegetation and contains mainly decaying plant and animal matter.

The tropics lie between the Tropic of Cancer and the Tropic of Capricorn (latitude 23.5° north and south). It is only in this zone that the sun is directly overhead with the result that temperatures are always high (except in highland areas) and the seasons are marked by changes in wind and rainfall. These conditions are ideal for vegetation growth and consequently the greatest rainforests in the world lie within ten degrees of the Equator. The most well known are the Amazon rainforest of Brazil, the Congo basin of Central Africa and the jungles of Malaysia, Indonesia, Burma, and Vietnam. In moist tropical rainforests it rains nearly every day and is hot and humid throughout the year. In the interior it is damp and dark and the trees grow up to 196 feet tall as they compete to reach the light and form the well-known rainforest canopy.

SUBTROPICAL CLIMATES

The subtropics refers to the zones of the Earth immediately north of the Tropic of Cancer and south of the Tropic of Capricorn, roughly between 23.5° and 35° north and south. These areas typically have very warm to hot summers, but non-tropical winters. A subtropical climate implies that the air temperature usually does not fall below freezing (32°F) and includes the regions of coastal California, southern Florida, northern India, coastal Australia, and coastal South Africa. Subtropical regions don't usually have distinctly wet or dry seasons, and have a fairly even distribution of rain throughout the year.

The climate in California ranges from subtropical to subarctic. and much of the state has a Mediterranean climate. In coastal California, summers are generally hot, and winters are mild and humid. Summer temperatures can exceed 90°F, and smog can be a problem. In winter, temperatures dip to an average of 55°F and rain is a possibility.

DESERT REGIONS

Deserts are made in different ways, but are always formed because there is not enough water. Desert landscapes have certain distinctive features and are often composed of sand and rocky surfaces. There are three main types: sandy deserts or ergs, rocky deserts or hammada, and stony deserts or reg. Deserts also sometimes contain valuable mineral deposits, formed in the arid environment or exposed by erosion. Because deserts are dry, they are ideal places for human artifacts and fossils to be preserved.

Hot deserts and semi-desert regions occupy one-fifth of the world's land surface. Deserts are dry, barren places that receive an average annual precipitation of less than 10 inches. They usually have an extreme temperature range and can have high daytime temperatures of over 122°F due to the intense heat of the sun and the lack of clouds. Even though the desert is very hot in the day, it is extremely cold at night because the air is very dry and therefore holds little heat; as soon as the sun sets, the desert cools quickly. Also, cloudless skies increase the release of heat at night. Deserts have a reputation for supporting very little life, but in reality they are often home to a high diversity of animal life; many of these remain hidden during daylight hours to control body temperature or to limit moisture needs.

TEMPERATE GRASSLANDS

There are vast areas of grassland in the interiors of the continents in the temperate zone. They develop where there is too little precipitation for trees to grow and the climate can be summarized by hot summers and cold winters, averaging 10–20 inches of rain, or equivalent in snowfall, a year. The soil is considered too moist to be a desert, but too dry to support normal forest life. Various names are given to these grasslands, including prairie, steppe, and pampas. These areas may be semi-desert, or covered with grass or shrubs, or both, depending on the season and latitude. Many kinds of natural grasslands are now becoming rare. About two-thirds of the Canadian prairies and half the United States prairies have been converted into huge cereal farms and there is little natural vegetation left. Much of the South African veld has also been destroyed.

The North American prairies, sometimes called the Great Plains, reach from Canada's prairie provinces almost to the Gulf of Mexico, and eastward to south of the Great Lakes. Herds of pronghorn antelopes and bison used to feed on these prairies before they were hunted close to extinction by 19th-century settlers. The American Bison, or buffalo, the largest terrestrial mammal in North America, are nomadic grazers and travel in herds on the Great Plains.

MEDITERRANEAN CLIMATES

The Mediterranean climate is ideal for growing many fruits, especially grapes, melons, and citrus; many of these areas are important wine producers. Olives have been grown in these regions for centuries and provide oil in areas where milk and butter are hard to produce. Vegetables also thrive, and often more than one crop a year is possible, especially where irrigation is available to supplement the meager summer rainfall.

Despite its name, this climate is not peculiar to countries fringing the Mediterranean Sea. There are Mediterranean climates between 30° and 40° north and south of the Equator. During the summer, warm dry winds blow from the Equator, bringing dry conditions. In the winter the winds swing towards the Equator and westerly winds bring rain. Summers are hot, and winters are usually warm enough for plants to grow. Frost and snow are rare except over mountains. In the area around the Mediterranean, the sea has a substantial effect on the climate: in the summer it is cooler than the land, so the air sinks down over the sea and the surrounding area and there is very little rain. Few clouds mean high temperatures. In the winter the sea is warmer than the land, so the surrounding land enjoys mild winters while the warm, moist air from the sea brings rain.

TEMPERATE CLIMATES

The temperate regions of the world lie between the tropics and the polar circles—in the latitudes of the changeable westerlies. The changes in these regions between summer and winter are generally subtle—warm or cool, rather than extreme burning hot or freezing cold. However, a temperate climate can have very unpredictable weather. One day it may be sunny, the next it may be raining, and after that it may be cloudy. These erratic weather patterns occur in summer as well as winter. In temperate zones, latitude and the shelter provided by hills or mountains have the most marked effect on average temperature and rainfall. However, all these regions have a dormant season when the temperature is below 43°F and plant growth ceases. Conditions are generally favorable for abundant plant and animal life and approximately 80 percent of the world's population live in temperate zones.

Temperate climates include northern Europe, British Columbia, Oregon and Washington State in North America, southern Chile, Tasmania, and South Island, New Zealand. Although temperate zones only account for about seven percent of the world's land surface, they are by far the most popular areas in which to live.

SUBARCTIC CLIMATES

Most of Alaska has a subarctic climate. Winters are very long, lasting—from late September to mid-April and are very cold and dry, with snowfall averaging approximately 67 inches a year. The extreme climate ensures it is one of the least populated American states.

This climate is peculiar to the Northern Hemisphere where the largest continents of the world extend into the Arctic Circle. Regions having a subarctic climate are characterized by long, very cold winters, and brief, warm summers. This type of climate offers some of the most extreme seasonal temperature variations found on the planet: in winter, temperatures can drop to –40°F and in the short, hot summers the temperature may exceed 86°F. With six to seven consecutive months where the average temperature is below freezing, all moisture in the soil and subsoil freezes solidly to depths of many feet. The frost-free season is very short and the warmth of summer is insufficient to thaw more than a few surface feet, so permafrost prevails under large areas. Vegetation in the subarctic climate consists almost entirely of conifers, which survive extreme cold and are not easily damaged by snow.

POLAR CLIMATES

The harshest climate on Earth occurs within the Arctic and Antarctic Circles. These regions are cold, icy deserts where it is bitterly cold all year round. The lowest temperatures recorded are in these areas—the record being −129°F at Vostock, a Russian research station in the Arctic, in July 1983. The northern polar region is an ocean basin surrounded by land. Floating ice covers much of the Arctic Ocean all year round with ice so thick that even the strongest ships cannot reach the North Pole. In warmer parts of the Arctic lands, ice and snow disappear in summer and tundra plants grow on the stony ground. The Antarctic region around the South Pole includes a huge continent almost covered with ice and snow. A deep ocean partly covered by floating ice, even in summer, surrounds it. Antarctica has such a harsh climate that people have never settled there permanently.

During the summer months in the polar regions, many types of small plants and millions of insects enjoy their brief life cycle, especially in the Arctic as migratory birds fly in. Year-round natural inhabitants are mostly restricted to seals, sea lions, and penguins in the south, and polar bears in the north. There is no farming, but fishing grounds yield high catches in the summer as the ice retreats.

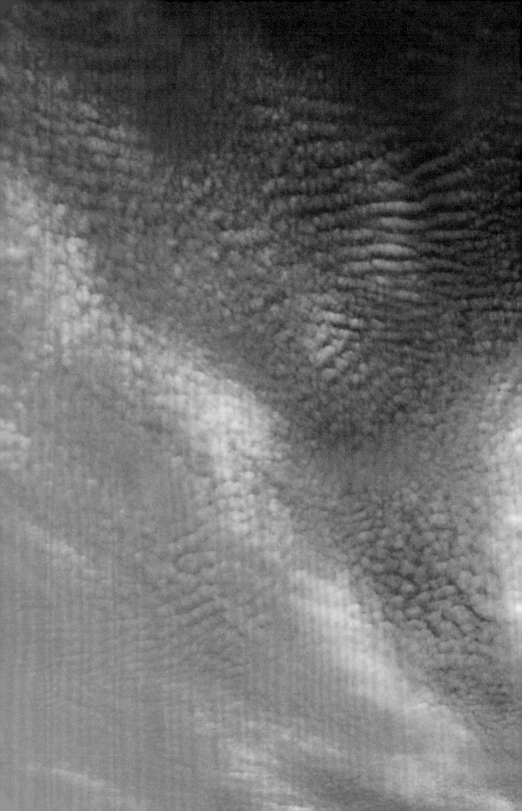

THE ATMOSPHERE: GLOBAL PATTERNS

THE CAUSES OF WEATHER

Other local aspects of physical geography such as valleys or coasts can have an impact on local weather: river valleys may experience fog more frequently than other areas and coastal areas generally experience cooler temperatures in summer and milder in winter than areas further inland. They may also be windier due to the impact of sea and land breezes. In addition to the impact of the natural environment, anthropogenic factors—human activity—are now of increasing concern.

The weather we experience at the Earth's surface is caused by a complex set of interrelated factors. Some of these are large-scale, affecting all parts of the Earth at some, or for most of the time. These include the impact of solar heating—energy from the sun and the tilt of the Earth on its axis in relation to the sun, in other words the seasons. Other large-scale, global factors include the amount of water vapor and other gases in the atmosphere which influence global temperatures. Additionally, the impact of high and low pressure systems and large scale permanent or periodic ocean currents is of fundamental importance in explaining particular weather and climate patterns. Other factors affect only relatively small areas of the globe and are more localized in their impact. These may include altitude, local winds or whether the area is rural or urban—urban areas can develop their own microclimates.

THE SUN

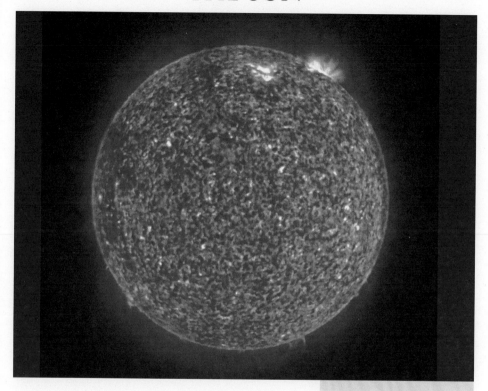

The sun provides the energy which drives the Earth's weather systems. The energy comes from the thermonuclear reactions taking place at its core. About 46 percent of the sun's energy is in the form of visible light. A similar amount is in the form of infrared radiation—heat. The remainder is ultraviolet radiation, the cause of sunburn in humans. Additionally, solar eruptions called prominences and flares occur periodically and give off considerably more energy and are believed to have significant temporary effects on our weather. The sun's surface (photosphere) has a temperature of about 5700 Kelvin (K), 9800°F, compared with 15 million K (27 million degrees F) at the core.

The sun is a huge ball of hydrogen gas, ionised into a plasma by the immense temperatures that are generated by nuclear fusion at its core. This fusion is ignited by the immense pressure generated by the sun's mass. An active sun is more likely to eject plasma from its surface and the level of activity varies, peaking roughly every 11 years. The sun's light and heat directly or indirectly provides almost all of the energy for life on Earth, despite being some 93 million miles distant from Earth.

THE SEASONS

Winter in the United States, when the Northen Hemisphere is tilted away from the sun. The days are cooler and shorter and the sun appears lower in the sky.

As the Earth makes its orbit around the sun there are changes in the amount of sunlight received which affects the temperatures experienced. The Earth spinning on its axis makes a single rotation every 24 hours, in other words, it creates a day and a night. It takes 365.25 days for Earth to complete a single orbit of the sun. As the Earth is tilted on its axis—23.5°—different parts of the world receive different amounts of sunlight at different times of year. At the Equator there is little variance in sunlight and thus in length of day and temperatures, there are no significant seasons. The Earth's tilt means that as it orbits the sun, the Northern and Southern Hemispheres are oriented either further toward or further away from the sun, with the result that the sun appears higher or lower in the sky, for longer or shorter periods, and its rays are experienced more or less directly or obliquely.

SOLSTICE AND EQUINOX

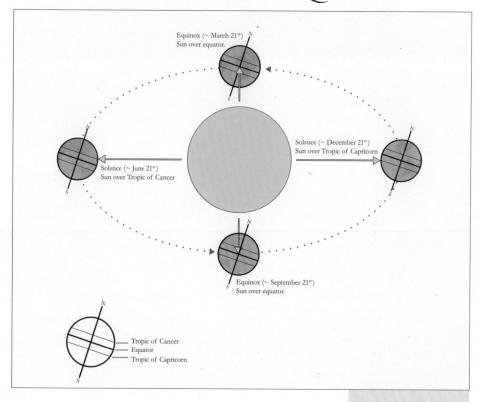

Equinox (~ March 21st)
Sun over equator.

Solstice (~ December 21st)
Sun over Tropic of Capricorn

Solstice (~ June 21st)
Sun over Tropic of Cancer

Equinox (~ September 21st)
Sun over equator.

Tropic of Cancer
Equator
Tropic of Capricorn

In the Northern Hemisphere the longest day, the summer solstice, is on June 21. This coincides with the winter solstice or shortest day in the Southern Hemisphere. These periodic variations in the amount of sunlight received, and the temperatures experienced, are delineated as the seasons. In the polar and temperate regions, the astronomical year is divided into four equal parts by the two solstices, when the sun is at its extreme northern and southern declinations, and the two equinoxes, when the sun traverses the celestial equator. The solstices mark the longest and shortest days of the year, whilst at the vernal and fall equinoxes, day and night are of equal duration. At any particular time of the year, each hemisphere is experiencing the opposite season so that the longest day in the Northern Hemisphere coincides with the shortest day in the Southern Hemisphere, and vice versa.

The four seasons, which are described as spring, summer, fall, and winter, are, in astronomical terms, divided by the vernal and fall equinoxes, and by the summer and winter solstices, with each marking the end of one season and the beginning of the next. However, in meteorological terms, the seasons are taken to begin around three weeks prior to these occurrences.

THE EARTH AS A SYSTEM

A color-coded infrared view of the Earth made by a Meteosat weather satellite. The colors represent temperature, from blue (coldest) to red (warmest). Blue features are tops of large cloud banks. Lower, and thus warmer, clouds are shown in yellow and pink, particularly across the center of the frame. Red areas are generally seas and oceans seen through breaks in the cloud. Land areas, such as the Sahara Desert and North Africa (yellow/green, above center), are often cooler than surrounding seas during the night as a result of radiative heat loss.

The Earth can be considered as a system in which all components interrelate. These components are the atmosphere (air), lithosphere (land), cryosphere (ice), biosphere (plants and animals) and hydrosphere (water). The system begins with the inflow of energy from the sun. It ends with the outward flow of energy back into space, so preventing the Earth from overheating. In between these inward and outward flows, the energy warms the planet drives the atmospheric engine and the water cycle. The latter is the process by which water changes between liquid, solid and gaseous states. Some other chemicals, such as carbon dioxide, also move through the cycle.

THE ENERGY CYCLE

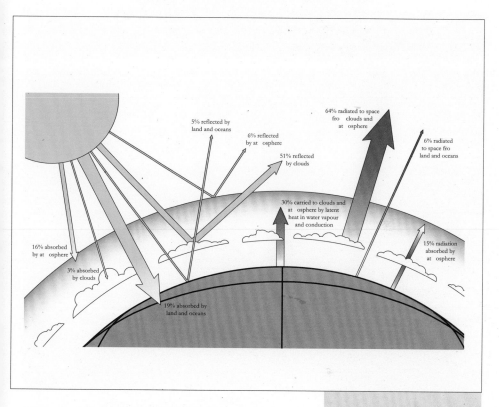

5% reflected by
land and oceans

6% reflected
by at osphere

51% reflected
by clouds

64% radiated to space
fro clouds and
at osphere

6% radiated
to space fro
land and oceans

30% carried to clouds and
at osphere by latent
heat in water vapour
and conduction

16% absorbed
by at osphere

3% absorbed
by clouds

15% radiation
absorbed by
at osphere

19% absorbed by
land and oceans

The sun provides the energy which drives the atmosphere, affects temperatures and so creates our weather. Incoming solar radiation—energy—enters the Earth's atmosphere. Some is able to reach the Earth's surface, heating it. The warmed Earth in turn heats the atmosphere above it. Some energy is absorbed and reflected by the gases in the atmosphere. Some energy returns to space. Some is used to evaporate water which subsequently condenses and cools to form clouds. These in turn absorb and reflect more energy. It is the constant recycling of the solar radiation received that fundamentally causes our weather.

Radiation from the sun reaches the Earth and is then absorbed by the atmosphere and surface of the planet. A proportion of this radiation is reflected back into space. Gases such as carbon dioxide trap some of this reflected radiation, with the result that the average surface temperature increases. This is known as the green-house effect because the layer of carbon dioxide has a similar effect to the glass in a green-house, which lets heat in and traps it inside.

ATMOSPHERE

Scientists have divided the Earth's atmosphere into four zones based principally on their temperature, density and chemical composition. The troposphere, closest to the surface, is the densest part of the Earth's atmosphere. The stratosphere is less dense and is also warmer because it aborbs much of the sun's radiation, thus providing a protective blanket for the Earth. The mesosphere is cooler than the stratosphere, but temperatures in the thermosphere rise dramatically with proximity to the sun and reach around 3100°F.

The atmosphere around our planet is critically important for our survival. It absorbs the energy we need, reflects the surplus back into space and provides a layer of protection against the harmful elements of incoming radiation. It contains gases, clouds, particles of dust, and other particles called aerosols; the main gases being nitrogen and oxygen. Arranged in distinctive layers with no clearly discernible outer limit, most of the atmospheric mass lies below an altitude of 62 miles. Compared to the Earth's dimensions, the atmosphere is very thin: the equivalent of a layer of skin to an onion. In recent years concern has grown over the potentially harmful changes believed to be taking place in the gaseous composition of the atmosphere.

ATMOSPHERIC LAYERS

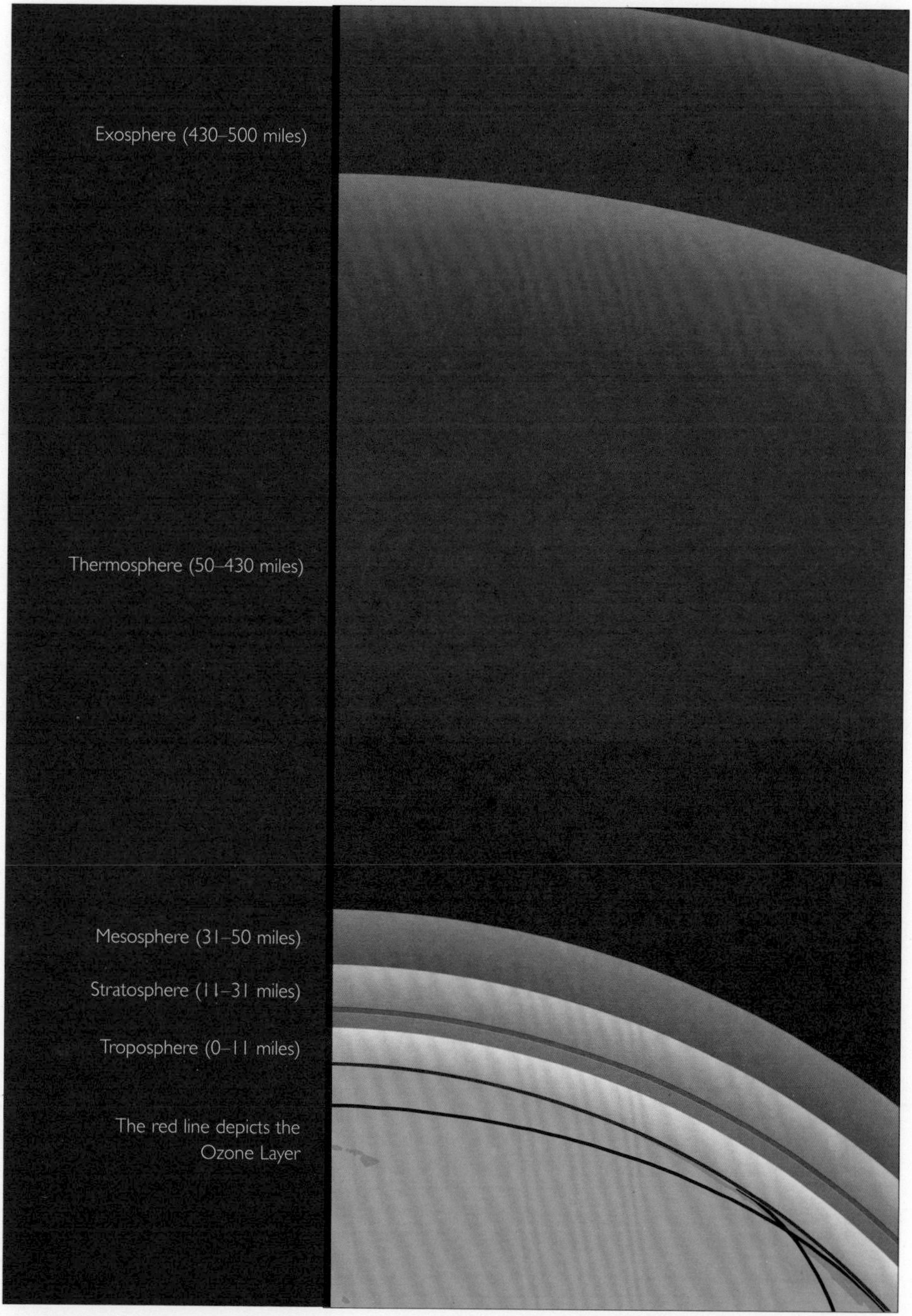

Exosphere (430–500 miles)

Thermosphere (50–430 miles)

Mesosphere (31–50 miles)

Stratosphere (11–31 miles)

Troposphere (0–11 miles)

The red line depicts the
Ozone Layer

THE TRADE WINDS

Global Wind Patterns

◄ Polar Easterlies

➤ Westerlies

◄ North East Trades
  & South East Trades

The theoretical movement of winds should be N–S but in reality they move in a generally NE direction. This is due to the Coriolis force set up at the Earth's surface as it spins on its axis. Above these cells and somewhat separate from them are the jet stream winds.

Because the Earth's surface heats up unevenly, there are varying bands of airflow which produce different weather at different locations. Between the Tropics there is relatively even, intense heating which produces powerful convection currents in the air. When air rises the resulting pressure at ground level is lowered. As the air here is warm, it rises, hence the low pressure. This occurs in a belt all around the globe. The air that has risen eventually reaches the troposphere, can go no further and so cools and descends in the region between 30° N and S. The air that has risen is replaced by air moving from about 30° N and S. The resulting circulation is known as a Hadley cell, after the 18th-century scientist who first suggested the idea. These cells give rise to the trade winds which carry warm air away from the Equator. The area at the Equator where there is little wind is the doldrums. At lower latitudes, air continues to rise and fall towards the poles, in a circulatory motion. These are known as Ferrel cells and these carry cool air toward the Equator.

THE CORIOLIS EFFECT

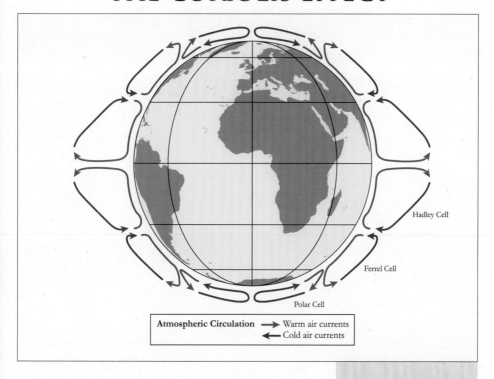

Hadley Cell

Ferrel Cell

Polar Cell

Atmospheric Circulation ⟶ Warm air currents
← Cold air currents

The Coriolis effect is caused by the rotation of the Earth. The effect deflects objects moving along the surface of the Earth to the right in the northern Hemisphere and to the left in the southern Hemisphere. As a consequence, winds around the center of a cyclone rotate anti-clockwise in the Northern Hemisphere and clockwise in the Southern Hemisphere. If the Earth's surface were smooth, uniform and stationary, atmospheric circulation would be very simple. Unequal heating is the main driving mechanism responsible for the Earth's atmospheric circulations and gives rise to the three cell circulation model: Hadley, Ferrel, and Polar cells.

The Hadley cell is a simple conveyor belt type of circulation pattern that dominates the tropical atmosphere and is related to the trade winds, tropical rainbelts, subtropical deserts, and the jet streams. The Ferrel cell describes the surface flow in the temperate zone of air that becomes the Westerlies (prevailing winds between 30° and 60° latitude). The Polar cell is the northernmost cell of circulation between 60°N and the North Pole and produces winds that are often weak and irregular.

THE JET STREAM

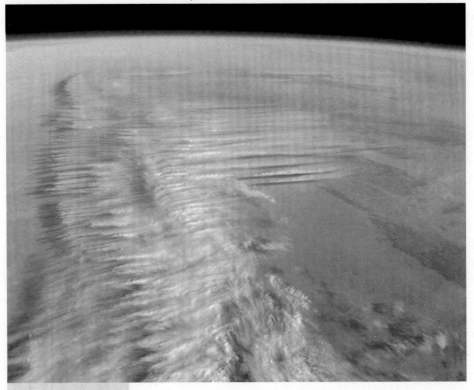

Jet stream clouds seen over north-western Libya. They are high-altitude, fast-moving air currents that are a hundreds and even thousands, of miles long. Cirrus clouds form at these high altitudes and are swept along in the jet stream. The jet streams form as a result of thermal effects, forming at the boundary between a warm and a cold body of air.

The upper atmosphere contains large, vertical cells of wind which rotate. These help to redistribute heat away from the Equator. They are usually stable but occasionally break up and reform; they have been associated with unusual weather such as drought and flood. In such circumstances the normal movement of low pressure is believed to have been dragged north by the jet stream. Air temperature decreases from the Equator to the poles and wind speed in the upper air is proportional to the rate at which temperature changes. This is most extreme where the equatorial and subtropical air masses meet, which is at the polar front, and where equatorial air meets tropical air. In these areas, narrow belts of wind—jet streams—blow, often with great force, between 100 and 150 miles per hour and sometimes in excess of 200 miles per hour.

AIR MASSES

Because the Earth does not heat up evenly, some places will be warmer than others. These sections of air can often cover huge areas of the Earth's surface, even as large as entire continents. Such areas of air are called air masses and have more or less the same temperatures, pressure and humidity. These air masses inevitably move, as warm air rises and is replaced by colder air. An air mass is called continental (dry) or maritime (moist) depending on whether it was formed over the land or sea. It is either polar (cold) or tropical (warm) depending on the latitude where it formed. Where air masses of different temperatures meet they form fronts, imaginary lines drawn on weather maps, which are more properly called synoptic charts. This situation is typical of that which causes depressions, low pressure systems, to form.

Northern Cape, South Africa. In summer, much of southern Africa is affected by maritime tropical air which is characterized by high temperatures, high humidity of the lower layers over the oceans and stable stratification. Since the air is warm and moist near the surface, stratiform cloud commonly develops as the air moves poleward from its source.

AIR PRESSURE

This isobaric map of western Europe shows a depression over Great Britain, surrounded by several anticyclones. The map consists of lines of equal air pressure (isobars). The air pressure in the depression falls towards the center of its tightly spaced isobars. The air pressure in the anticyclones rises towards the center of their widely-spaced isobars. They bring settled dry weather with light winds. Isobaric maps are used for accurate weather forecasting.

Atmospheric or air pressure is the weight of the air on the land. It is measured in millibars using an instrument called a barometer. The barometric pressure is recorded both locally and globally and when places of the same pressure are joined together with lines called isobars and shown on a map, a complex pattern emerges. Distinct areas of high and low pressure appear which, on a global scale, appear in well-defined bands which largely coincide with latitude. When air is warmed by the Earth's surface it rises, reducing the pressure on the land surface. Conversely, air at altitude is cooler than that below it so descends and increases the pressure on the Earth's surface.

PRESSURE SYSTEMS

Satellite image of low-pressure off Australia's southern coast. Land is brown, water is dark blue and clouds are white. These systems develop when a pressure difference between the core and its surroundings, combined with the Coriolis effect, causes air to circulate. The resulting swirling clouds, seen at center, rotate in a clockwise direction in the Southern Hemisphere.

Air naturally moves from high to low pressure. Imagine a toy balloon filled with air: the air inside is under considerable pressure as it is trapped inside the rubber skin of the balloon. Undo the knot at the end and the air inside rushes out toward the area of lower pressure outside. The movement of air from high to low pressure is, of course, wind. High and low pressure areas are associated with distinctive weather. High pressure creates dry and calm weather which can produce periods of drought or, in winter, frosty conditions. In contrast, low pressure is associated with cloudy, windy and wet weather. Areas of extreme low pressure may develop into tropical storms called hurricanes or typhoons. Given the exceptionally close association of air pressure with weather, pressure systems are closely monitored by forecasters.

HIGH PRESSURE

A cloudless area of high pressure, an anticyclone, lies over the British Isles. Swirling clouds mark the position of a depression or cyclone, an area of low atmospheric pressure, in the Atlantic Ocean at upper left.

Air pressure means the weight of the air on the Earth's surface. If the air pressure is high it means that cold air must be descending and adding weight—pressure—on the ground. This air then warms up as it reaches the lower levels of the atmosphere; the air molecules expand, becoming larger than water vapor molecules which are then absorbed. This means the air is dry—no clouds. The air is calm or has light winds but what wind does exist will blow in a clockwise direction in the Northern Hemisphere and the reverse in the Southern Hemisphere. High pressure systems are often known as anticyclones.

HIGH PRESSURE CONDITIONS

Distinct weather occurs under high pressure conditions. In the summer the characteristic light winds or calm conditions and lack of cloud means the weather is dry and sunny—ideal summer weather. The lack of rainfall, however attractive it may be for holiday-makers and for farmers at harvest time, can be a problem as drought is a characteristic feature of persistent high pressure. In the winter the weather conditions are broadly the same as in the summer— dry, calm and with clear skies. A bright, crisp winter's day may be ideal for a country walk but there is a sting in the tail of such weather. The lack of cloud cover creates exceptionally cold temperatures, particularly at night. Any heat generated during the day radiates out into the atmosphere and, with no cloud to trap the heat, frost is likely.

Namaqualand, South Africa. When high pressure lies overhead, conditions tend to be quiescent with light and variable winds. Locations close to mountain ranges often experience variable conditions over a relatively short time because mountains cause air to rise, enhancing cloud formation and precipitation.

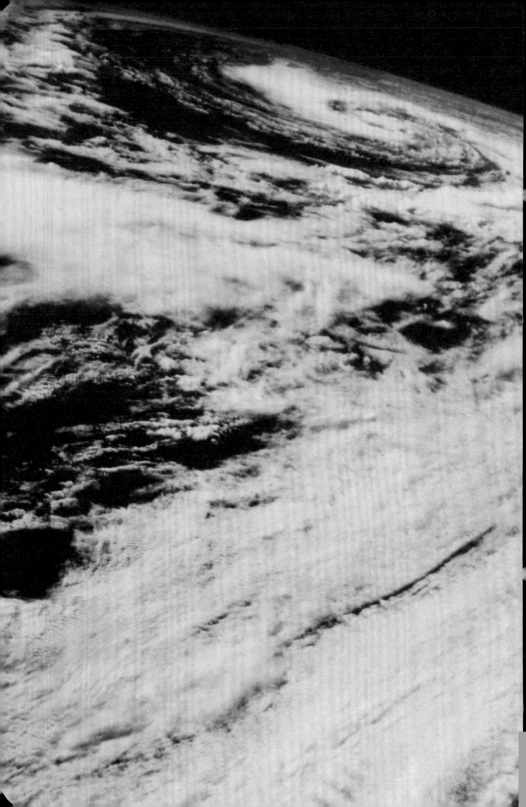

LOW PRESSURE

Wet, windy, often cold and dull weather is inevitably the result of low atmospheric pressure systems, or frontal systems as they are often termed. These are common in mid-latitudinal belts around the globe where they may also be known as depressions or cyclones. When seen from space they are identified by the distinctive swirl of cloud which brings rain and dull weather. In extreme cases, the low pressure may intensify to form hurricanes, also known as tropical cyclones or typhoons.

Depressions form where two air masses of different temperatures meet. When they do they meet along an imaginary line called a front which is identified by a swathe of cloud. The cold air is dense and heavy whereas the warm air is lighter. When they meet, the warm air mass rises over the cold air as it is lighter. As it rises it creates an area of low pressure into which the cold air moves; the advancing edge of this is the cold front. The rising warm air creates cloud and, if conditions are right, rain. The fronts begin to rotate upward and outward as the air rises because of the Coriolis effect, brought about by the Earth's rotation on its axis. The air rotation is anti-clockwise in the Northern Hemisphere and the reverse in the Southern Hemisphere.

Storm clouds seen from the Challenger Shuttle in space. This photograph shows the clouds associated with a cyclonic disturbance. This is found near a low pressure region, and used to be called a mid-latitude cyclone. If the depression at the center of the storm has a very low pressure, it may lead to relatively violent storms with high winds. The center of this system is seen as the spiral of clouds just below the Earth's limb near top center.

DEPRESSIONS

A cyclone is a system of winds rotating inward to an area of low barometric pressure. The cyclone forms the swirl of clouds surrounding the "eye." Cyclones can form into hurricanes or typhoons. The "eye" comprises relatively calm, cloud-free air at a very low pressure. Around this "eye" are the cyclone's strongest winds.

A depression or low pressure system is formed when a cold air mass meets a warm air mass. Common in mid-latitudinal areas both north and south of the Equator, they are responsible for a great deal of the annual precipitation that falls across these areas and can produce very wet and windy weather. A typical depression will take about 48 hours to develop and finally disperse before re-forming later, a process called cyclogenesis. The weather that is typical of a depression will vary depending on which particular air masses are involved but will have common characteristics.

LOW PRESSURE CONDITIONS

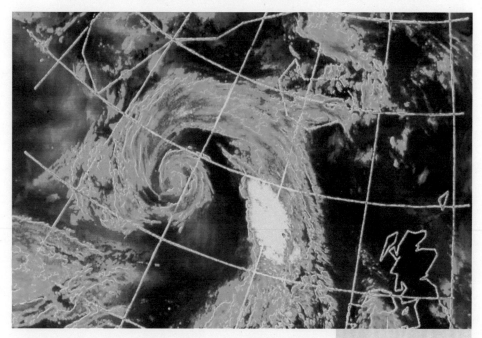

As the warm front advances, air pressure gradually falls, temperatures remain steady and wind speed increases, backing slightly. Conditions become increasingly overcast and so visibility falls as cirrus clouds are replaced with alto- then nimbostratus clouds. As the front moves overhead the winds veer, temperature and humidity rise markedly and the earlier continuous, heavy rain eases or stops. At this point the area behind the warm front but ahead of the cold front is known as the warm sector.

As the cold front advances, air pressure falls a little and wind speeds increase but temperatures fall significantly. Cloud cover is low, stratus and altostratus, making visibility poor and bringing light rain, which increases markedly as the cold front passes overhead; hail and thunderstorms could occur. Once the cold front has passed, air pressure gradually rises; wind veers and decreases in speed. Temperatures remain low, visibility improves and shower clouds replace the low, heavy, dull conditions; bright intervals, interspersed with showers, now dominate weather conditions.

A colored satellite image of a low pressure frontal system over the North Atlantic Ocean. The system is the swirling mass of clouds (at center). Low-level clouds are shown as yellow and red, high-level clouds as white. In a low pressure system, the air pressure decreases toward the center of the spiral of clouds.

FRONTS

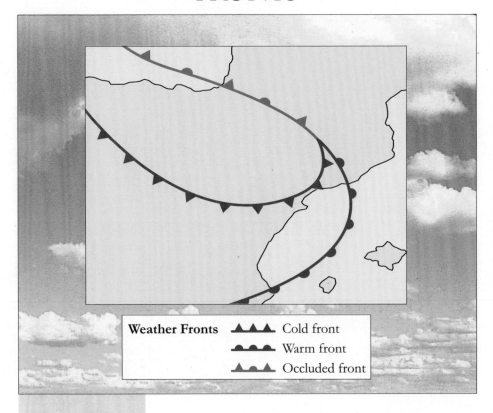

Weather Fronts ▲▲▲ Cold front
━●●●━ Warm front
▲●▲ Occluded front

Diagram showing the symbols for cold, warm, and occluded fronts. A warm front has filled semi-circles, whereas the cold front has filled triangular barbs. An occluded front is shown as a mixture of cold and warm fronts and has both semi-circles and triangles alternating along the line.

A front is an imaginary line drawn on a weather map, more appropriately called a synoptic chart, and it marks the point at which a cold air mass meets a warm air mass. Fronts form an important part of a low pressure system or depression. There are three different types of fronts— cold, warm, and occluded. Each one is represented on a synoptic chart as a solid line with the different types of front having a special symbol added to identify them. The three different fronts may exist within the depression depending on the conditions that develop. Once formed, depressions are carried east in the Northern Hemisphere along the Rossby Wave system.

TYPES OF FRONTS

The cold front marks the advance of the cold air mass and dense cold air moves beneath warm air, forcing it to rise. The lifting of the warm air causes cooling, condensation and cloud formation and may produce showers, perhaps thunderstorms. At a warm front, warm air rises up and over a cooler, denser air mass. This forms an area of thickening cloud which gradually reaches lower altitude creating dull, wet conditions. In the picture above the line of clouds is associated with a cold front and marks the boundary between two air masses of differing temperature. As the squall line passes overhead there is a sudden rise in wind speed, often associated with other violent changes in weather conditions. A veer in wind direction, a rise in pressure and a drop in temperature accompany the passage of the front. Occluded fronts occur when a cold air mass catches up with a slower-moving warm air mass. and they become uplifted. This leaves more uniform air at the surface and eventually leads to the decay of the system. Over the course of about 48 hours the denser cold air behind the front pushes beneath the warm air, catches up with the warm front and forces the warm air off the surface. The effects of the warm front are lost and any rain that forms is unlikely to be heavy.

View of an approaching dry squall line. A squall line will usually develop ahead of and parallel to a cold front. A squall is a sudden, sharp increase in wind speed over a short time interval.

SEA AND LAND BREEZES

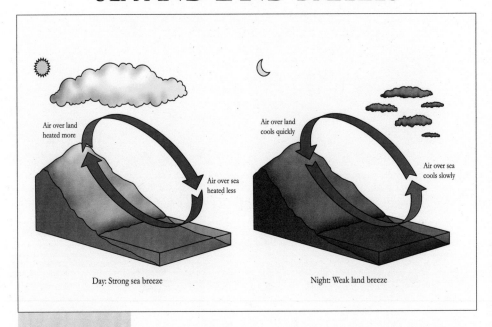

Day: Strong sea breeze

Night: Weak land breeze

Air over land heated more

Air over sea heated less

Air over land cools quickly

Air over sea cools slowly

As the land heats up in the daytime, the wind comes from the sea, but at night the sea retains heat longer so the wind changes direction.

There are distinct reversals in wind direction during the day and overnight. This is brought about by the diurnal heating and cooling of the Earth. As the surface heats up, it causes thermals to form as the warmed air rises, and stronger upper-level winds are brought down to the surface to replace it. Overnight the Earth's surface rapidly loses heat, most notably if the skies are clear with no insulation from clouds. Temperature inversions may form, where temperatures at altitude are higher than those at ground level, and winds below the inversion become light and variable. Soon after the sun rises, the ground is heated and so the cycle repeats itself. Sea breezes are a common feature of coastal locations and they form because of this variability of heating and the resulting air movements—winds. During the day the land heats up faster than the sea. Air pressure falls over the land as the air rises and cooler air rushes in from the sea to replace it, and a wind forms—sea breeze—which normally reaches its peak in the late afternoon. Overnight, however, the land cools more quickly than the sea. The surface air, which is cooler than that over the sea, sinks and drains off the land and out over the ocean.

MONSOON WINDS

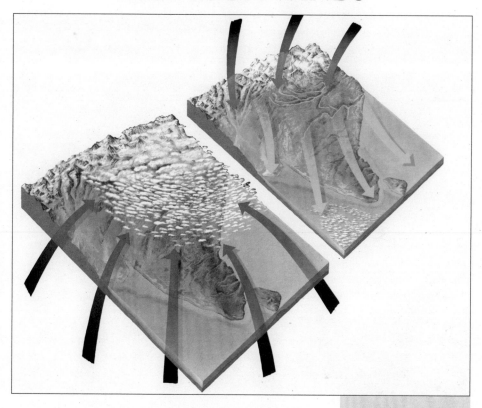

This diagram represents the monsoon winds in summer (left) and winter (right) in southern Asia. In summer, the land heats up much faster than the ocean, and the hot air rises, causing a large area of low pressure. This draws in the cooler, moister air from the ocean, producing a steady wind from the south-west. Clouds form as the moist air hits the Himalayan mountain range, producing a huge amount of rain, which is vital for crops but often leads to flooding. In winter, the situation is reversed: the sea cools more slowly than the land, thus the low forms over the ocean. This draws cool air from the mountains, forming a wind that blows from the north-east. In Cherranpunji in India, the average rainfall in January is 0.75 inches but in July the rainfall peaks at 96 inches.

Monsoons are seasonal changes in wind, usually bringing heavy rain, that are experienced in many of the world's tropical regions such as India, Bangladesh, and Pakistan. A monsoon is a land and sea breeze on an enormous scale, which is produced by seasonal changes in atmospheric pressure systems.

WATER

The coast near Arniston, South Western Cape, South Africa. Ocean currents have a huge impact on the weather experienced over nearby lands. The air above cold currents carries little moisture, which helps to create deserts on the west coasts of continents. The contrast between cold ocean temperatures and the warm land also produces sea breezes along these coasts.

Almost 90 percent of all the water on Earth is stored in the oceans, rivers, and lakes—the hydrosphere. After that, the largest store of water is in the form of ice in the world's glaciers or ice sheets—the cryosphere. Sea water comprises 97 percent of all water on Earth; the only fresh water on Earth is the remaining three percent. Of that fresh water 77 percent is stored as ice. The remaining water is either in the lithosphere—underground, stored in aquifers (22 percent of the fresh water)—or in the atmosphere. Only one percent of all freshwater occurs in the form of water vapor, soil moisture, rivers, lakes, and inland seas.

THE HYDROSPHERE

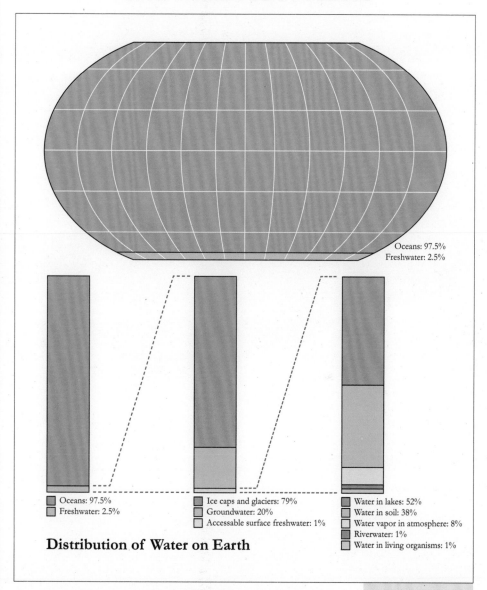

Oceans: 97.5%
Freshwater: 2.5%

☐ Oceans: 97.5%
☐ Freshwater: 2.5%

☐ Ice caps and glaciers: 79%
☐ Groundwater: 20%
☐ Accessable surface freshwater: 1%

☐ Water in lakes: 52%
☐ Water in soil: 38%
☐ Water vapor in atmosphere: 8%
☐ Riverwater: 1%
☐ Water in living organisms: 1%

Distribution of Water on Earth

The water in the seas is of particular global meteorological importance since the oceanic currents redistribute the warm or cold water through the so-called "great conveyor belt" which is believed to drive the world's weather engine.

Diagram showing the distribution of water on Earth.

THE WATER CYCLE

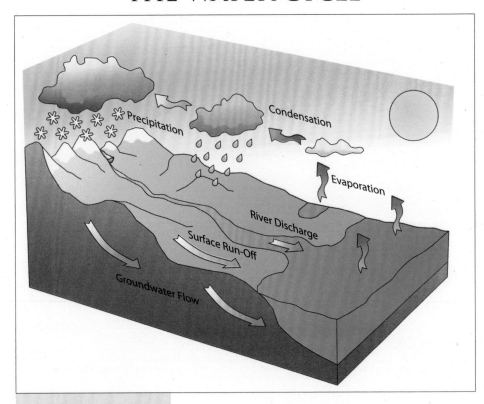

Diagram giving an overview of the water cycle. Water evaporates from the ocean and may fall as precipitation over land (lower left, top). Water re-enters the atmosphere from land by evaporation and transpiration (water loss by plants) (top). Water flows from land to ocean in surface rivers and streams (center). It also travels through soil and rock as groundwater (right).

The relationship between water in all its forms and the way it is transferred from one state or place to another is the water or hydrological cycle. It is the basic mechanism by which water is moved, and exists because air absorbs and releases water vapor. The cycle can begin with evaporation from a surface such as the sea. Onshore winds will force the resulting water vapor to rise and if the temperature drops enough it might reach dew point—saturation point. Condensation of water vapor into clouds will then occur with some precipitation resulting. When it reaches the ground a number of different things may happen.

Some of the precipitation will infiltrate the underlying rocks and could be stored as ground water in aquifers if the right geology—porous rock such as chalk—is present. Some will be absorbed by the soil and may flow through under the influence of gravity to reach the sea once more. Some may fall as snow and over time develop into glacial ice to be largely stored until some future date when evaporation and melting takes place, changing the ice back into a liquid. Some may be stored in rivers, lakes, and inland seas from which more evaporation can take place. Vegetation is another way in which falling precipitation may be used within the cycle. Plants take up the water for growth and transpire the surplus from leaves. Alternatively they may intercept precipitation on their leaves which is later evaporated and returns to the water cycle.

Water tumbles over Burnley Falls, California, USA. Water is constantly redistributed by a variety of processes.

HUMIDITY

Aqua satellite map of water vapor in the atmosphere over the oceans. The amount of water vapor is color-coded, from light blue (least) to dark blue (most). The small yellow areas correspond to areas of high precipitation. Snow and ice are yellow and deserts are dark green. Other land is black.

Humidity is the amount of water vapor, a colorless gas, in existence in the atmosphere. A high humidity means there is a lot of water in the atmosphere. How humid the atmosphere is depends on where the air has come from and its temperature, and so it will vary considerably between places. At the poles there is no humidity, but in the tropics it can be as much as four percent by volume. As the air temperature increases water molecules evaporate, some eventually condensing to form a liquid. When equilibrium develops between the evaporation rate and the condensation rate saturation or dew point is reached and so the air can hold no more water vapor. At this point, deposition of water takes place on surfaces or in the atmosphere.

Water vapor is another greenhouse gas, one that absorbs energy that would otherwise escape into space and so causing the earth's temperature to increase. Interestingly, when the air warms it has an increased ability to hold water vapor and so more heating takes place and so on.

DEW AND FROST

The dew that appears on the lawn and the frost that appears on windshields on winter mornings is the result of air close to the Earth's surface being saturated with water vapor. During the day the ground is heated by incoming solar radiation which in turn heats the air. At night, however, the ground cools rapidly, particularly if the sky is clear. The air in contact with the ground cools but the air above is warmer (air is a good insulator). The air at or near the ground cools to saturation at the dew point, the temperature at which water vapor starts to condense. When the saturation point is above the freezing point of water (32°F) dew will form but if it is below freezing point it is frost that will form.

When the forecasters refer to a ground frost it is one in which the ground is frosty but the air temperature is still at three or four degrees. An air frost is one where temperatures in a Stevenson's Screen reach zero even though the ground sometimes remains above freezing point. This is common in fall as the ground retains a little warmth from the summer.

There are two types of frost. Hoar frost (shown above) forms when the air cools and water condenses onto the grass in a delicate icy structure. It only forms when winds are very light and creates a definite, delicate crystalline structure growing on elements in steps or layers. Rime occurs when frost formation occurs quickly and is common during fogs, where near-freezing water droplets come in contact with freezing surfaces. It has a grainy appearance and is denser and harder than hoar frost.

CLOUD FORMATION

Warm, moist air rises and as it cools at higher altitudes, water vapor condenses and forms clouds.

A cloud is a collection of water droplets or ice crystals that are packed together densely enough to make it visible. Water vapor needs a nucleus in the atmosphere for condensation or accumulation to take place. This is usually something in the atmosphere such as dust and is called a hygroscopic or condensation nucleus. The study of clouds is called nephology.

Clouds form where water vapor is cooled to saturation—the dew point. This is then followed by condensation, leading to the formation of water vapor droplets or deposition of ice crystals. Temperature falls with altitude—the lapse rate. At high altitude all clouds are made of ice crystals but at low altitude they are composed of water droplets.

Clouds can be associated with convection, mechanical (orographic), or dynamic uplift. Convection means that warm air becomes increasingly buoyant compared to the surrounding air and rises. Mechanical or orographic uplift occurs when air moves over mountains and dynamic uplift refers to large-scale air movement into low pressure systems or along fronts. Essentially, clouds form where there is uplift, cooling and condensation.

CLOUD TYPES

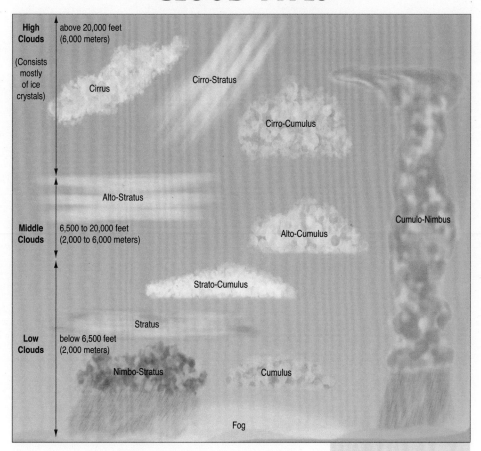

High Clouds — above 20,000 feet (6,000 meters)
(Consists mostly of ice crystals)

Cirrus

Cirro-Stratus

Cirro-Cumulus

Alto-Stratus

Middle Clouds — 6,500 to 20,000 feet (2,000 to 6,000 meters)

Alto-Cumulus

Cumulo-Nimbus

Strato-Cumulus

Stratus

Low Clouds — below 6,500 feet (2,000 meters)

Nimbo-Stratus

Cumulus

Fog

Clouds can be classified according to form and altitude on what is sometimes called a "cloud atlas." According to the World Meteorological Organization there are 10 types of cloud. These are classified according to the altitude at which they develop and the form or shape that they take. There are two basic types of cloud: layer or stratus cloud which covers the sky completely and is associated with stable air conditions; and heap cloud— clumps of cloud—usually cumulus.

There are ten basic cloud types:
Cirrus
Cirro Stratus
Cirro-Cumulus
Alto-Stratus
Alto-Cumulus
Cumulo-Nimbus
Strato-Cumulus
Stratus
Nimbo-Stratus
Cumulus

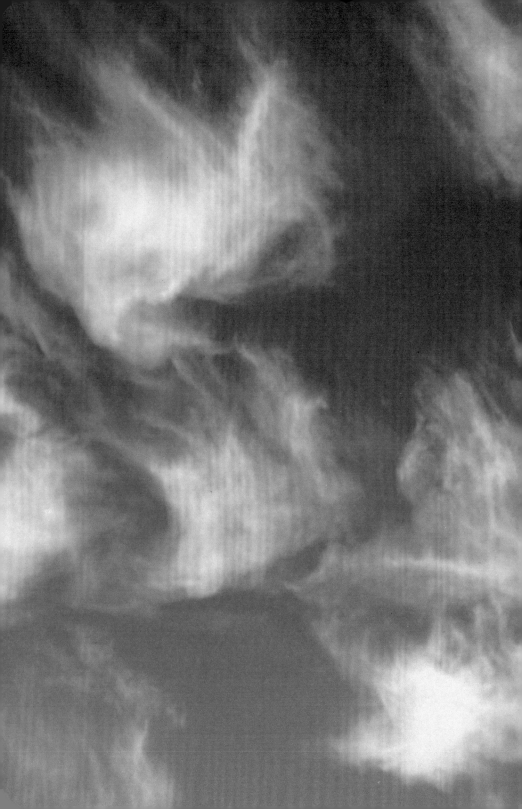

HIGH-ALTITUDE CLOUDS

These are largely composed of ice crystals and their base should be at or above 12 miles.

Cirrus

These form at or above 12 miles but that altitude is lower at the Poles because of the lower temperature. They are formed of ice crystals and have a feathery or wispy form.

Cirrostratus

These are layer clouds which cover most of the sky. They usually herald bad weather and sometimes form a halo around the sun or moon.

Cirrocumulus

These are ice clouds usually with irregular attractive patterns. They are a heaped form of cirrus.

Scattered plumes of cirrus cloud in the sky. Depending on their shape, these clouds are also known as "mare's tails" or "stringers." Cirrus is a high-altitude ice crystal cloud which forms delicate filaments or fibers. This cloud type is usually associated with fair weather.

Cirrus is a high-altitude cloud, formed of ice crystals. It appears as delicate white filaments, patches, or streaks. The long streaks with feathery ends have the common name of "mare's tail." Isolated cirrus is sometimes known as an emissary sky, as it often heralds an approaching cyclonic storm.

Cirrus Kelvin-Helmholtz cloud with its distinct corkscrew pattern is formed by layers of air moving across each other in opposite directions, creating a series of circular air movements in between them. This type of cloud generally forms at high altitude and dissipates rapidly.

Above: "mare's tail" cirrus cloud.

Opposite Below: Cirrus (top), cirro-cumulus (in main cloud layer) and cumulus (low on the hills) cloud types visible over the Himalayan foothills of east Nepal.

Opposite Above: Spiraling cirrus Kelvin-Helmholtz cloud.

MEDIUM-ALTITUDE CLOUDS

These develop at heights between 8000 and 18,000 feet.

Alto-cumulus
These are flattened globes or globules of cloud which are a mixture of ice and super-cooled water. They are white and gray in color and are often the first sign that thunderstorms will follow.

Alto-stratus
As the name suggests, these are layer clouds of a dull gray color and quite often make the sun have a milky appearance. They are often the first sign that rain is to follow.

Nimbo-stratus
These are thicker, lower versions of altostratus and are always associated with rainfall or snow. They can, however, be so thick and dark that they make the day appear very dark.

Above: Alto-cumulus clouds tend to be larger and darker than high-altitude cirro-cumulus, and smaller than the low-altitude strato-cumulus.

Opposite:
Alto-cumulus clouds lit up by the setting sun.

LOW-ALTITUDE CLOUDS

These are water clouds whose bases form at 6500 feet.

Strato-cumulus
These clouds are composed of water and are gray and white with darker areas inside. Their appearance is rounded and rolled.

Stratus
Water clouds which are gray in color, these form uniform layers which bring drizzle or snow. They are the lowest clouds in the sky and in fact form "fog" if over hills or coasts.

Cumulus
These heaped clouds are often described as "cauliflower-like" in appearance. They are gray at the base and white at the top.

Cumulo-nimbus
These are the classic anvil-headed thunder clouds which can reach as high as 40,000 feet into the atmosphere. This high up in the upper atmosphere the tops of the clouds are icy.

Above: Cumulo-nimbus clouds are large, turbulent clouds which carry rain or hail.

Opposite Above: "Fair-weather" cumulus are small clouds of no great vertical extent and are associated with mild weather. Cumulus may be produced at a frontal system boundary or as a result of thermal cell activity, with a low-altitude cloud base at between 1000 and 3300 feet.

Opposite Below: Cumulus clouds in Botswana.

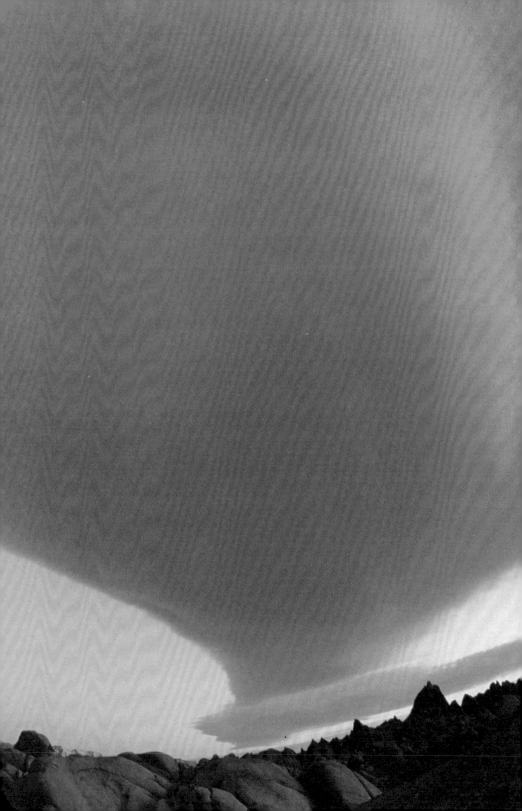

LENTICULAR CLOUDS

As air moves over isolated hills or mountains it is forced to rise to go over them. As it does so the water vapor in it cools to dew point and condenses forming clouds. The clouds that develop are hump-backed or lens shaped, hence lenticular, and normally develop at right angles to the wind direction. Some mountains are almost permanently shrouded by such a cloud, for example peaks in the Himalayas and Table Mountain in Cape Town, South Africa which is frequently covered by the lenticular cloud known locally as "the tablecloth."

Left: Fish-eye view of a lenticular cloud (alto-cumulus lenticularis) over Sandstone Bridge, Alabama Hills, California, at sunset.
A lenticular cloud gets its name from its smooth, lens-like shape. When wind blows across mountains it tends to cause waves on the mountain's lee side. Lenticular clouds form when moisture in the air condenses at the top of these waves. If the mountain has a regular shape and the wind blows at a constant speed, the cloud pattern will be stable, have a regular shape and remain virtually stationary in the sky for long periods. The Sandstone Bridge is a natural arch formed by weather erosion.

Above: Lenticular clouds are sometimes mistaken for alien "flying saucer" spacecraft.

MOTHER OF PEARL OR NACREOUS CLOUDS

A nacreous or mother-of-pearl type of polar stratospheric cloud (PSC). PSCs are high-altitude icy clouds that are found about 15 miles up in the polar stratosphere. They only form during winter when the temperature drops below −112°F.

These are very high-altitude clouds, formed at heights of up to 20 miles in the stratosphere and mesosphere. They are rare, seen only at dawn or dusk when the Sun is about 5° to 10° below the horizon, and look similar to high cirrus. At this angle the sun illuminates the clouds to stunning effect, creating beautiful mother-of-pearl-like colors. They do not appear to move and are probably formed as a result of rapid uplift of air over a mountain range.

NOCTILUCENT CLOUDS

These are fast moving clouds which form at extremely high altitude, at about 36 miles, at the top of the mesosphere and above the height of satellites. They are visible only during the summer between about 50° and 65° north and south and, like nacreous clouds, are seen when the sun is between 6° and 12° below the horizon while the ground and lower layers of the atmosphere are in shadow. They are very fast-moving and although their formation is still unclear, it is believed they are associated with the jet stream, hence speeds of 300 mph.

Noctilucent clouds (white streaks across center) are very thin and form high above the Earth at heights of 47–56 miles. Because they are so thin and high, they can only be seen at twilight, shining in the glow of the setting sun, and only at high and low latitudes. The lower three layers of the atmosphere (from bottom) are the troposphere (orange, 9 miles thick), and the stratosphere and mesosphere (both pale blue and 28 miles thick). Above these, the atmosphere fades into the darkness of space.

MOUNTAIN WAVE

Mountain Waves.
As air moves over isolated hills or mountains it is forced to rise or go over them. As it does so the water vapor in it cools to dew point and condenses forming clouds. The clouds that develop are hump-backed or lens-shaped and normally develop at right angles to the wind direction.

When air blows over a hill or mountain it first has to rise to overcome the obstacle of the hill itself and then it falls down the leeward side. This motion is wave-like in character. Each time the air rises it reaches dew point and cloud formation takes place. The cloud then disperses as the air falls down the leeward side of the hill. Despite the air movement the cloud that has formed appears stationary. This is a form of lenticular cloud.

CONTRAILS AND DISTRAILS

The path left by aircraft engines is a contrail, sometimes called a vapor trail—effectively man-made clouds. As the plane flies it releases water vapor and gases that condense rapidly in the cold air. Low pressure can form small eddies at the aircraft wingtips leading to water vapor condensing or freezing, causing smoke-ring-like effects along the contrail.

Contrails are artificial clouds formed from frozen water droplets from the exhaust of the engines of an aircraft. They form when aircraft are flying at altitudes exceeding 116,000 feet and when the upper atmosphere is nearly saturated with moisture. In dry air the contrail quickly disperses. Sometimes these "chromosome-shaped" patterns form as the contrail dissipates.

FOG

Fog and mist are, essentially, clouds formed at ground level. Like clouds, mist and fog are formed when water vapor is cooled to dew point and condenses. Both are made of tiny water droplets in suspension in the air with the difference between them being the density of droplets. The officially accepted definition of fog is when there is visibility of less than 3300 feet, but a more conventional definition is where visibility is 650 feet or less. This happens when there is a high density of water droplets in the air. When visibility falls below 165 feet severe disruption to transport occurs with significant risk of accidents.

Radiation fog is the most common type of fog. The ground absorbs heat during the day but at night it radiates outwards cooling both itself and the surrounding air. If it cools enough then some water vapor may condense into cloud droplets on the ground and form fog. Ideal conditions are slight winds which are needed to stir up the cold air and create condensation across the wider area, clear skies and long nights.

The rusty red twin towers of the Golden Gate Bridge, San Francisco, rise out from the dense advection fog. Fog comprises tiny droplets of water. It forms when relatively warm, moist air is cooled. As it cools, some of the water vapor in the air condenses to form water droplets. This is because cool air can carry less water vapor than warm air.

TYPES OF FOG

A false-color satellite image of north-west Europe, showing a large fog bank in the North Sea. The British Isles and the coasts of northern Europe and Scandinavia are seen clearly. Thin, high-level clouds are seen over parts of Germany and Austria.

Advection fog is formed when very warm moist air blows over a cold surface. The lower layers of air are cooled down to a level at which condensation occurs, creating fog. The characteristic fog over the Golden Gate Bridge in San Francisco in California, USA is formed in this way. Moist onshore winds blow across the cold water of the Pacific during the summer months. Hill fog is formed as mild moist air flows up the windward side of a slope where it cools and, if the air is saturated, condenses. If this occurs below the hill top it forms fog. Coastal fog forms when a warm stream of air passes over cold water cooling the lower layers of air below dew point. This type can be seen to be literally coming in on the tide. Freezing fog is composed of super-cooled water droplets that remain liquid even if the air temperature is below freezing point. Smog is a mixture of smoke and fog: air pollution creates ideal conditions for the formation of water droplets and when these mix with pollution caused by burning fossil fuels a thick, noxious fog is created. The infamous London "pea-soupers" of the 19th and early 20th centuries are typical examples of urban smogs.

PRECIPITATION

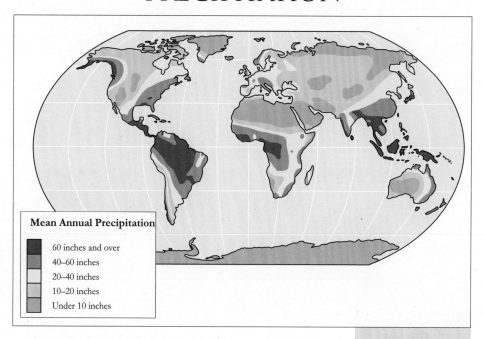

Mean Annual Precipitation

- 60 inches and over
- 40–60 inches
- 20–40 inches
- 10–20 inches
- Under 10 inches

Any liquid, or frozen liquid, that falls from the atmosphere to the Earth's surface under the influence of gravity is classed as precipitation. Precipitation is hugely important as it keeps water circulating between the various stores in the atmosphere, oceans, glaciers and ice caps, lakes, and rivers. There are three types of precipitation classified according to their state: liquid (water), solid (ice) or freezing (snow or hail). Only those clouds that are at least 4000 feet deep will cause precipitation to occur. Nimbus and cumulo-nimbus create the heaviest precipitation. Some clouds will cause precipitation which does not always reach the ground surface. A typical raindrop contains a million times more water than the average cloud droplet and the fastest raindrops can fall at about 30 feet per second. In contrast, snow only falls at 1.5 to 3 feet per second.

Many parts of the world receive virtually no precipitation of any form. In the northern Atacama desert of Chile the town of Calama received no rain for 400 years. All that changed in 1972: torrential rainfall occurred, causing flooding, landslides and a great deal of damage to the town.

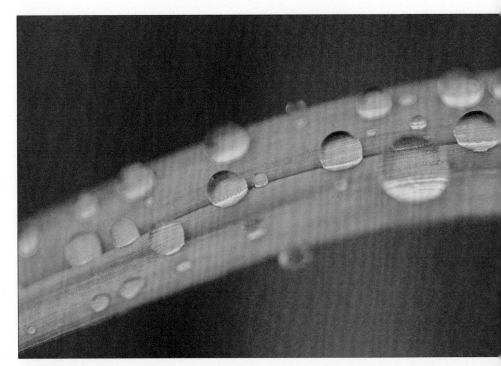

RAIN

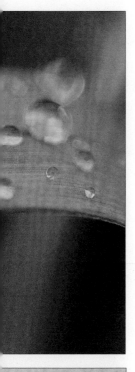

This is the liquid form of precipitation. When rain clouds are sufficiently deep they will produce large drops which fall as rain. This can vary from very light or showery conditions to extremely heavy rain which can lead to flooding. Drizzle is in the form of a fine mist-like precipitation which appears to drift slowly in the air. Its impact is slight—more an irritation to pedestrians and drivers than anything else—and may not be enough to be measured in a rain gauge. Rain clouds can form through any one of three main processes: orographic rain clouds form over hills and mountains, while frontal rain clouds form where two air masses meet; rain clouds also form when convection causes warm, buoyant air to rise.

The process by which rain forms is not simple. The Bergeron–Findelson effect, named after its Swedish and German proponents, is one of the most important theories of rain formation. It explains the complex interaction between water vapor, super-cooled water droplets and ice crystals at temperatures between 14°F and –4°F. This allows larger crystals to form which eventually fall out of the clouds as snow. As the crystals descend the air temperature increases, the snow melts and turns to rain. In tropical areas, however, the air temperature is usually too warm for ice crystals to form therefore the rain that falls in these areas is the result of coalescence, in other words the raindrops collide and eventually form large enough drops to fall to Earth as rain. In thinner cloud conditions, the drops will collide with fewer others and so form smaller drops, creating a fine mist—drizzle.

Above: Falling raindrops are often depicted as teardrop-shaped in cartoons or drawings. In fact this is only true when they are dripping from a surface. Small raindrops are spherical. Larger ones become increasingly flattened on the bottom and very large ones are shaped like parachutes.

Below: View of distant rainfall in Death Valley, California, USA. The shower can be seen (lower center) as a gray/pink sheet of rain emerging from cumulus clouds. Rain is extremely infrequent in Death Valley. This rain fell as an effect of the 1998 El Niño event in the Pacific Ocean some distance to the west.

SNOW

For most children—and many adults—snow is the most exciting type of precipitation and is eagerly anticipated as winter develops. Some people still believe that snow is frozen rain but it isn't. Snow forms when tiny ice crystals collide and stick together. Most snow crystals melt as they fall to the earth but when the air is cold enough they remain and the snowflakes fall as snow. When it is very cold snow crystals tend to be drier and powdery because the ice crystals do not find it easy to stick together. This is the snow that skiers particularly relish and snow forecasts highlight this as ideal for skiing. The intermediary stage, when some of the falling snow has melted but the precipitation lands as half-snow and half-rain, is sleet.

Heavy snow along a creek during a snowstorm in Missouri. Snow is made up of large ice crystals which grow inside clouds from smaller crystals. When it is very cold, snow forms small, dry flakes, making powder snow on the ground. In warmer temperatures larger, wetter flakes are created.

SNOWFLAKES

Snowflakes are symmetrical ice crystals that form in calm air with temperatures near the freezing point of water. The exact shape of a snowflake depends on local climatic conditions. Snowflakes typically have hexagonal symmetry, as seen here. No two snowflakes are identical, as each experiences a wide range of conditions as it forms inside a cloud.

Each snow crystal has a unique structure and pattern. This depends on temperature, altitude and the saturation of the clouds as they form. They join together when they are wetter and then re-freeze; so large flakes tend to form when the air is relatively warm, just above freezing. This situation also tends to develop the heaviest falls as warm air can hold more moisture. Incidentally, this type of snow is the best for those children (and adults) who want to make—and throw—snowballs! The Inuit people have several different words for snow as they recognize, and indeed need to understand the significance of, the numerous types that form.

HOW HAIL IS FORMED

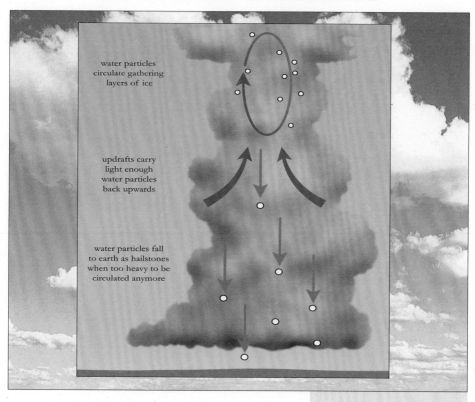

water particles circulate gathering layers of ice

updrafts carry light enough water particles back upwards

water particles fall to earth as hailstones when too heavy to be circulated anymore

Associated with thunder storms and often with tornadoes, hail is an interesting weather phenomenon for most people. For others it is livelihood-threatening and it can kill: 246 people died during a hail storm in Moradabad, northern India in 1888. Were you able to slice through a hailstone you would see that it is layered rather like an onion. This layering is a clue to the hailstones beginning as an ice crystal in an unstable cloud such as cumulo-nimbus or storm cloud and associates hailstorms with violent downpours and storms. Within the cloud there are strong vertical air currents which throw the ice crystals up and down in the cloud. Eventually the hailstone becomes so heavy that it cannot remain suspended in the cloud and it falls to the ground.

Hail is a form of precipitation made up of balls of ice. The hail forms in cumulo-nimbus clouds due to violent convection currents. Particles of rain or snow are drawn vertically up through the cloud, and collide with super cooled water and other particles. These collisions lead to the particles sticking together. When they become too heavy to be supported by the air currents, they fall to the ground.

HAILSTONE DAMAGE

Shaft of hail pouring from a severe thunderstorm in Gillette, Wyoming, USA. Some hailstones can be over 4 inches across, and cause severe damage to property and crops.

Hailstorms are unwelcome because of the damage they inflict on crops and homes. In the central states of the USA is an area known as Hail Alley where millions of dollars of damage occurs every year when hailstorms arrive. The force of the landing hail flattens crops, often making them unrecoverable. In other parts of the world, such as Italy, farmers lay out matting roofs on scaffolding poles to help protect vulnerable fruit on trees from the damaging effects of hail. In Sydney, Australia, an area not normally noted for severe hailstorms, one occurred in 1999: in a storm lasting less than 15 minutes, hailstones, varying from golf to cricket ball in size, fell at speeds of up to 100 mph severely damaging 25,000 homes, making 44,000 homeless.

HAILSTONES

A typical hailstone is around 0.2 inches in diameter but even for one only this size, it is necessary for there to be strong winds—100 feet per second. Although not very common, it is not rare to find golf-ball-sized hailstones falling. Much rarer are the considerably larger hailstones such as the one which fell during a storm in Kansas in 1970. This weighed 27 ounces was (17.2 inches) in circumference and almost 6 inches inches diameter. An even larger hailstone fell in Gopalganj in Bangladesh in 1986, weighing in at a hefty 2½ lbs.

Colored image of a giant irregularly shaped hailstone 6 inches across. Hailstones are lumps of ice formed in storm clouds (cumulo-nimbus) when water droplets remain fluid after their temperature has fallen below freezing point. This super-cooled water circulates in the updrafts within the cloud, forming ice on contact with dust particles in the air. The hailstones grow larger as they circulate around the cloud until they are either too heavy for the cloud to support or are thrown out of the updraft area.

THE ATMOSPHERE: LOCAL PATTERNS

CONTINENTAL CLIMATES

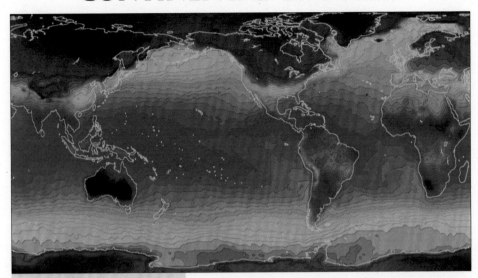

A satellite map of the world's average surface temperature. Colors represent temperatures as follows:

Mauve = –36°F;

Blue = –33 to 10°F;

Green = 14 to 32°F;

Yellow = 36 to 39°F;

Pink and red = 61 to 93°F;

Deep red and black (as in Australia) = 97 to 104°F.

The Steppes of Russia and the Prairies of North America conjure up images of huge expanses of grassland. Both areas are far distant from the moderating influence of the sea and so have developed a continental climate. The sea has a high specific heat capacity which means that it takes a long time to heat up and similarly a long time to cool down. The land, however, has a much lower specific heat capacity. When solar radiation reaches the land the soil and rock absorb energy in a shallow surface layer which heats up quickly and then cools down quickly. This means that continental areas have a very large temperature range, as much as 70°F in parts of the USA.

MARITIME CLIMATES

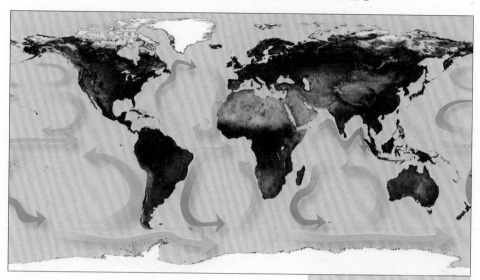

A maritime climate is moderated by the influence of the sea. Water has a high specific heat capacity which means that it takes a long time to warm up in the summer but retains heat for some time and so takes a long time to cool in the winter. The highest land temperatures occur in the summer months of July and August. The maximum sea temperatures, however, occur in September when the air temperatures are falling. This means that areas near to the sea benefit from the air blowing across relatively warm seas in the fall and winter so maintaining air temperatures across the land. Conversely, when continental areas swelter in very high summer temperatures, maritime areas benefit from the modifying cooling of the air blowing from the sea.

Computer artwork showing surface ocean currents. Warm water is red and cold water is blue. Surface currents are driven by the winds. At bottom is the eastward flowing Antarctic Circumpolar current. The Gulf Stream is a warm current that arises in the Caribbean Sea and travels up the Eastern coast of the USA before crossing the Atlantic. The trade winds drive the water westward along the Equator and at mid-latitudes the water is driven eastwards by the easterlies. These opposing winds cause the currents in the ocean basins to form gyres, or giant loops.

OCEANICITY

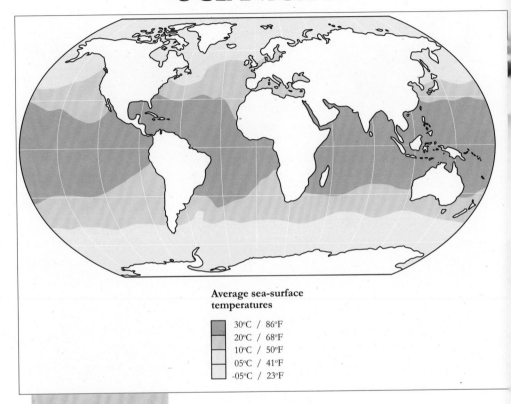

Average sea-surface temperatures

30°C	86°F
20°C	68°F
10°C	50°F
05°C	41°F
-05°C	23°F

Alaska and western Canada experience a maritime climate but, unlike the United Kingdom, they have no warm water current to keep temperatures up. The Gulf Stream keeps western Europe significantly warmer than it would otherwise be. The Circumpolar current is unobstucted by land for the entire circuit of the Earth and is the strongest of the surface ocean currents.

Oceanicity is a measure of the degree to which a region's climate is influenced by the flow of air from over the sea. A maritime west coast climate is typical of the west coasts of mid-latitude areas but is also found in a small part of south-eastern Australia. This climate type is characterized by cool and moist summers and mild winters, with a small annual temperature range. It has no serious extremes, unlike those of continental climate areas such as the Russian Steppes. The British Isles benefit from a moderate maritime climate as the prevailing south-westerly winds blow across the Atlantic. The maritime air masses from this direction are mild due to the warming effect of the Gulf Stream, a warm water current. In Britain the average annual temperature range is only about 18°F.

ALTITUDE

Anyone who has flown recently will have been able to monitor changing temperatures in the atmosphere as the aircraft climbs to its cruising altitude. Back down on the ground we can see similar decreases of temperature with altitude as we climb up a mountain side, for instance on a walk in the hills. The decrease in temperature is caused by increasing distance from the source of heated air—the Earth's surface. The atmosphere is warmed by the land which is itself heated by incoming insolation from the sun. Air is warmer nearer the Earth's surface as it is closer to the source of heat. The rate at which air cools or warms depends on how much moisture is in the atmosphere.

This decrease of temperature with altitude is known as the environmental lapse rate of temperature or normal lapse rate of temperature. The normal lapse rate, on a global scale, equates to 3.3°F in every 1000 feet; however, on any given day at any given location this may vary at which point it is called the environmental lapse rate.

Mountain cloud forming over a coastal mountain in the Arctic summer. This cloud is formed as a result of moist sea air rising to high altitudes when it meets the mountain. The water vapor condenses in the cold temperatures at these altitudes, forming orographic clouds. The resulting rain supports life in this otherwise arid desert of the Arctic.

OROGRAPHIC EFFECTS

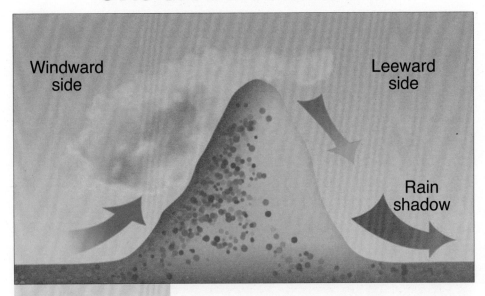

Windward side

Leeward side

Rain shadow

It is possible for hills and mountains to produce clouds by themselves. Some mountains develop lenticular clouds which are formed by locally rising air which condenses as it rises over the top of the hill. This air cannot rise further, however, and so the winds then "bounce" downstream of the mountains. These lenticular clouds do not move along with the wind but appear stationary. They form as the air rises and dissolve as the air descends hence the apparent stationary effect.

Those who live in hilly or mountainous areas are aware that the weather they experience is often different from that of the surrounding areas. This is what orography is, the effect of those hills and mountains on weather. As the wind blows over the sea it picks up moisture from evaporation. If the air is then blown onshore it is forced to rise when it reaches the hills. As it does so it cools and allows condensation to take place which causes the formation of clouds from which precipitation falls. Most rain falls on the hill tops or the windward side of the hills, the side facing the sea and so the onshore winds. As the air descends on the lee or sheltered side of the hills it warms; evaporation takes place and the air dries so little rain falls. This results in the leeward sides experiencing much drier conditions than the windward sides.

LOCAL WINDS

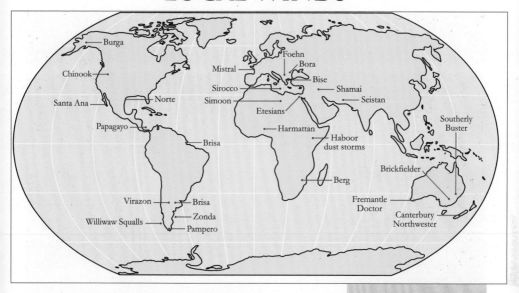

In many parts of the world the local geography such as mountain ranges, hills, and valleys can produce a wide range of local weather conditions including winds, sometimes seasonal and with potentially devastating consequences. Many of the winds have been given names which highlight the nature of the effects they bring. One of the most famous is the strong, cold wind that blows south off the Alps, the Mistral. This usually develops as a cold front which blows southward across France to the Mediterranean. It usually brings dry, colder summer weather and high seas. In the USA, the Chinook wind which blows off the Rocky Mountains marks the end of the winter's snow and heralds the start of spring. The Santa Ana wind of California blows during fall and spring and commonly reaches speeds of about 40 mph but when it flows between mountain passes it can approach hurricane force. In contrast, in an already windy part of the world, a cold wind blows from the Andes in a south westerly direction across Argentina's Patagonia district. This is the Pampero wind which brings stormy conditions and a significant drop in temperature.

The shape and topography of the land and sea in many parts of the world combine to form marked local winds which have been given special names over the years. The Chinook, in the United States brings hot and dry conditions in California and the Mistral causes windy conditions in the south of France.

MICROCLIMATES

A microclimate is a local external atmospheric zone where the climate differs from that of the surrounding area. Examples include the tropical rainforests. The temperature and humidity underneath the rainforest canopy will be very different from those of the surrounding external area.

"Microclimate" refers to the state of the atmosphere in a small area of the Earth's surface, perhaps a forest, town or even a garden. Natural microclimates occur widely such as in an area of forest. The treetop canopy in areas like the tropical rainforests of Brazil is thick and dense. This absorbs solar radiation and so develops very high temperatures. Beneath the canopy temperatures gradually decrease because of shading; in summer the temperature difference can be up to 40°F. Humidity levels and night-time forest temperatures are usually higher than those of the surrounding area and winds are light because of the protection from the canopy. Man-made microclimates are common: grand 19th century houses often had walled kitchen gardens which offered protection from wind; fruit trees and tender plants would have been grown against south-facing walls, absorbing solar energy during the day and re-radiating it at night, helping to maintain temperatures and assist ripening.

URBAN HEAT ISLANDS

Perhaps the most significant man-made microclimate is the urban heat island. As towns and cities have grown, so the difference in temperatures between them and the surrounding rural areas has increased. Brick and concrete buildings and dark tarmac surfaces absorb solar radiation during the day. At night this heat is released and warms the atmosphere. Heat from factories, air conditioning and refrigeration units, central heating and vehicle exhausts all add to the problem. Tall buildings also tend to trap the heat between them; roads and sidewalks do not retain moisture—it is channeled away by an extensive network of drains—so they remain warm. The temperature differential is obvious all year but is often more pronounced during the winter; in any case temperature differences of up to 18°F have been recorded.

Thermogram showing the distribution of heat over city buildings. The color coding ranges from yellow and red for the warmest areas (greatest heat loss) through pink to purple and green for the coolest areas (lowest heat loss). Typically roofs and windows show greatest heat loss. Thermograms are often used to check buildings for heat loss, so that they can be made more energy-efficient through improved insulation.

TEMPERATURE INVERSIONS

Aerial view of the anvil-shaped top, or thunderhead, of a cumulo-nimbus storm cloud. The thunderhead forms at the temperature inversion layer in the atmosphere, where the air above is warmer than the air below. The rising columns of moist, warm air which create cumulo-nimbus clouds are trapped by the inversion layer and so spread outward.

The normal pattern in the atmosphere is for temperatures to decrease with height. This is because the ground is heated by solar radiation which then warms the air above it due to radiation. Under certain conditions, however, the pattern is reversed and temperatures can be colder at ground level than in the atmosphere above it, creating a temperature inversion. There are several reasons why these may form. In California, citrus fruit growers worry about clear skies on winter nights since the day's relatively warm air can radiate away and temperatures may drop below freezing. Along the California coastline, wind blowing onshore may have moved across cold water causing its temperature to drop. When it reaches the coastline the cold, dense air cannot easily rise so displaces the lighter, warmer air, resulting in a temperature inversion.

Temperature inversions have been responsible for the persistence of smog over cities such as Los Angeles as vehicle exhausts and other sources discharge pollutants into the atmosphere. The cold, dense air of the inversion means that they are unable to disperse and are instead kept close to ground level. In valleys at night another type of inversion can take place: the air over hills is cold and, under the influence of gravity and because cold air is dense and heavy, it flows down into the valley where it displaces the relatively warmer air. The movement of the air is a katabatic wind, which is light and can often go unnoticed. The result is sometimes known as a frost hollow because the likelihood of frost in the valleys is very high.

Smog over Los Angeles, California, USA. This results from hydrocarbons and nitrogen oxides, mainly from vehicle exhausts, reacting together in the presence of sunlight. The pollution limits visibility, damages plants and irritates the eyes. High levels of smog can be extremely dangerous, especially to the very young and old, and those with existing respiratory complaints.

THE GREAT SMOG OF LONDON

Writing in *Bleak House* in 1853, Charles Dickens described the characteristic smogs of the city as "London Particulars," so common were they. They were not new; smogs, a mixture of fog and pollution, sometimes called "pea-soupers" because of their color and thickness, had existed since Elizabethan times and were referred to by the diarist John Evelyn in the 17th century.

During the immediate post-war period, not only was coal still the most common fuel burned in homes and power stations in the city, but diesel fuel was being used to run the buses that were replacing street cars as the main form of public transport. The early part of the winter of 1952 was particularly cold and people were burning more coal than usual to keep warm. The cold spell was due to a high pressure system which remained over the city from the start of December. London lies in a broad, shallow basin and a katabatic wind caused the very cold air from the surrounding hills to sink into the basin. The relatively warmer air over the city was forced upwards creating a temperature inversion. As the air in the inversion was calm and saturated, all the pollutants from factories, power stations, homes and transport were unable to be dispersed and mixed with the fog that developed at the same time.

Visibility fell to below 30 feet for almost 48 hours at Heathrow Airport, but in places people could not see their feet! Transport came to a standstill and a performance at the Sadler's Wells Theatre had to be canceled as it became impossible for the audience to see the stage and the performers to see each other. The emergency services and mortuaries were overwhelmed: at least 4000 people are known to have died, mainly as a result of bronchial or cardio-vascular conditions worsened by the smog. At Smithfield Cattle Market in central London it was reported that the animals were dying of asphyxiation. The death rate peaked at 900 a day on December 8 but over 2000 died in the week ending December 6 alone. Many researchers have since put the number of deaths unofficially at over 12000.

Following the smogs in the winter of 1952–53, the government was forced to take action and the Clean Air Act of 1956 was passed, making the "pea-soupers" a thing of the past. Despite the legislation, vehicle exhaust emissions remain a principal cause of London's urban pollution problems today.

URBAN POLLUTION

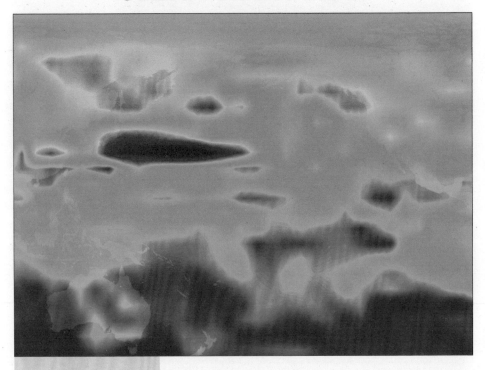

Satellite image of atmospheric carbon monoxide (CO) flowing east across the Pacific Ocean at an altitude of 1500 feet. Red indicates areas of high concentration (approximately 250 parts per billion) and blue indicates areas of low concentration (approximately 40 parts per billion). Carbon monoxide is caused by the incomplete combustion of carbon in, for instance, forest fires and engines. It is an important tropospheric (lowest region of the atmosphere) pollutant.

In 1948 the steel—and zinc—making town of Donora, Pennsylvania, suffered a serious industrial pollution incident which killed 19 people in just 24 hours. The small town of about 14000 people lies in a river valley and that October a temperature inversion resulted in a persistent fog developing which, mixed with the industrial pollutants released into the atmosphere, caused highly noxious smog to form. Of the 19 who died, almost all suffered from chronic heart disease or bronchial problems. Another 500 became ill from similar medical conditions which worsened during the two days at the peak of the smog, with as many as 7000 people believed to have been affected in total. The problem only eased after a temporary closure of the offending factories. Although not directly responsible, the event helped to put pressure on national and state government policy which eventually resulted in the Clean Air Act of 1970.

SEASONAL AFFECTIVE DISORDER

There is an increasing amount of evidence to suggest that the weather has an effect on our behavior. Lack of sunlight is believed to be the cause of "the winter blues" or Seasonal Affective Disorder (SAD). Sunlight stimulates the hypothalamus, that part of the brain that controls the body's main functions such as mood, activity, and sleep. If the body is not exposed to sunlight these functions slow down and people feel lethargic or depressed. It is in the more extreme latitudes that the numbers affected by SAD are highest; for instance Alaska, where research suggests that 10 percent of the population suffer compared with Florida with an estimated 1 percent.

Treatment is with sunlight—phototherapy—but since the reason so many are affected is because sunlight is absent, light boxes are used instead. Sufferers use them for several hours a day in order to counteract the effects of long winter nights.

A woman is reading a book as she undergoes phototherapy in front of a light screen. Phototherapy is used to treat jet lag and Seasonal Affective Disorder (SAD). SAD causes depression and withdrawal in winter months, as daylight time decreases. By exposing the patient to a strong light source for a few hours each day, the impression of longer daylight hours can be created.

WIND CHILL

The wind chill effect is the apparent temperature felt on exposed skin because of the combination of air temperature and wind speed. Except at higher temperatures, the wind chill temperature is always lower than the air temperature, because any wind increases the rate at which moisture evaporates from the skin and carries heat away from the body.

Wind chill is a measure of the amount of heat lost from the skin as the wind blows over it, in other words how much colder we feel the temperature to be as a result of the wind blowing. For instance, when the temperature is 32°F a 10 knot wind will make it feel as though it is 23°F. An increase in wind speed to 25 knots will cause the temperature to feel as though it is 10°F. The idea was developed to take into account the conditions likely to be experienced by those working in Antarctica. The obvious problem there is frostbite and research showed that wind speed was critical to the development of the condition. Scientists realized that it was quite possible to work in temperatures as low as −40°F but that it would only take a wind speed of 3 or 4 knots to make an enormous difference.

ADAPTING TO THE WEATHER

Plants and animals demonstrate a wide range of physical adaptations and behavioral strategies for surviving and thriving in particular environments in which the latitude and climate are major determining factors. Plants typically display adaptations in their leaves and roots, the forms of which may enable them to best obtain sunlight, retain moisture, survive extremes of temperature and humidity, protect them from severe winds, and allow them to thrive where nutrients are in short supply. The main concern for animals in relation to climate is probably that of temperature, which in ectothermic, or "cold-blooded" animals is governed by the temperature of their surroundings, and in endothermic, or "warm-blooded" animals, may be determined to an extent by the ambient temperature, but relies primarily on internal temperature regulation, which is achieved by processing carbohydrates and body fat.

Many species of tree adapt to the conditions of the climate of the places where they grow. The leaf stalks of many trees that grow in hot climates, such as the Australian and Pacific islands, and Africa, are vertically flattened; this helps to protect them from intense sunlight. In temperate climates, deciduous trees respond to winter by dropping their leaves.

TEMPERATE ADAPTATIONS

The needle-like leaves of conifers help to minimize water loss, and are protected against freezing by large spaces between their cells. The leaves of deciduous trees tend to be large and flat to maximize their exposure to sunlight, and are shed in the winter to prevent excessive moisture loss, at a time when water in the soil may be frozen.

In the temperate regions between the poles and the Equator, four seasons are experienced, presenting a variety of conditions that plants and animals must cope with, including warm, humid summers, and cold, often snowy winters, particularly in northern temperate zones, where freezing conditions may persist for much of the year. Rainfall tends to average between about 24–60 inches. Temperate regions tend to be dominated by deciduous broadleaf forests, comprised of trees such as oak, maple, birch, and beech; coniferous forests, consisting of cedar, spruce, cypress, firs, and other evergreen varieties; and mixed forests. Birds and mammals of temperate areas may migrate seasonally in winter in order to find more favorable conditions, whilst some mammals, reptiles, and amphibians, may hibernate. Many insects, however, typically die in the winter, having laid eggs during the summer and fall, which will hatch the following spring or summer.

POLAR ADAPTATIONS

The polar regions are characterized by extremely low temperatures, low rainfall, strong winds, and snow and ice. During the winter, there are long periods with little or no sunlight, whilst in the summer there are extended periods of daylight, although the sun remains low on the horizon, and temperatures only rise above freezing for a few months, perhaps reaching around 54°F at best. The dominant habitat is tundra: essentially frozen marshland or bog, with low-growing grasses, sedges, lichens, and mosses being the main forms of vegetation. Terrestrial fauna is limited in polar habitats, and is particularly restricted in the Antarctic, although there are several species of marine mammals that inhabit both polar regions, and which are protected against the cold by dense layers of fat or blubber. The Emperor Penguins of the Antarctic are able to withstand the coldest temperatures on Earth by huddling together in huge colonies, protected by dense layers of both feathers and blubber.

Penguins are particularly well adapted for life in the cold Antarctic waters. Their wings, shaped like flippers, help them swim underwater at speeds up to 15 mph. A streamlined body, paddle-like feet, insulating blubber, and watertight feathers all add to their efficiency when submerged. In addition to their blubber, penguins have tightly packed feathers that overlap to provide waterproofing; they coat their feathers with oil from a gland near the tail to increase impermeability.

ARID ADAPTATIONS

Camels are well-adapted to life in the desert. Their hump contains fat which can provide both their nutritional and water needs over prolonged periods. Their feet are wide, allowing them to walk on soft sand, and have thick soles to withstand the ground's heat. They are able to close their nostrils against airborne dust and their eyes are protected by thick eyelashes.

The arid and semi-arid regions of the world are defined by dry climates, where there is typically very little rainfall, although in semi-arid regions, where the main habitats are grasslands there may be wet and dry seasons. In truly arid habitats, however, the main biome type is that of desert, which may experience no rainfall during some years. Humidity is also very low, ensuring massive temperature variation on a daily basis, with the full force of the sun sometimes producing temperatures of over 122°F, and a lack of cloud cover at night meaning that temperatures can fall to −4°F. In the large deserts of the world, which occur mainly around the Tropic of Cancer and the Tropic of Capricorn, plant cover is very sparse; those plants that are present tend to be succulents, with fleshy, waxy stems and leaves designed to retain water, and extensive root systems in order to obtain it.

TROPICAL ADAPTATIONS

Tropical climates and habitats occur in the equatorial regions, bordered by subtropical regions to the north and south. Tropical regions experience high levels of sunlight, high temperatures and rainfall promoting the development of luxuriant rainforests, with incredibly high species diversity. Conditions in subtropical regions may be similar, but tend to experience more seasonal rainfall, leading to the establishment of monsoon forests, where plant growth may be limited by a shorter growing season, trees may shed their leaves during the dry season and animals may migrate to be close to sources of water. The warm, humid conditions in these habitats are ideal for many invertebrates, reptiles and amphibians. The dense vegetation also provides food and refuge for numerous birds and mammals, many of which feed on fruits, helping to disseminate seeds, and several birds and insects also pollinate flowers.

Many mosses, lichens, and ferns belong to a group of plants called epiphytes. These are plants which grow above the ground surface, using other plants or objects for support. These plants have adapted to life in climates such as a tropical rainforest, reaching positions where the light is better or where they can avoid competition for light.

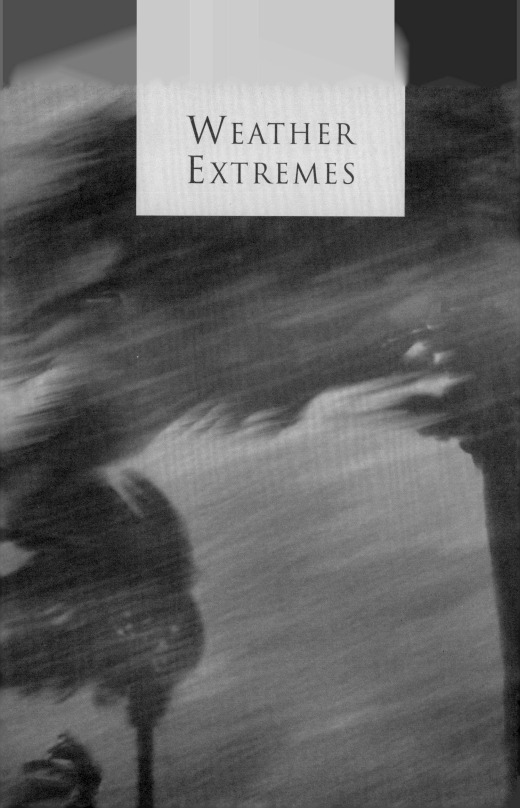

WEATHER
EXTREMES

STORMS

Storms are characterized by huge anvil-headed cumulo-nimbus clouds which can be between one and six miles across and may reach a height of 12 miles. Inside these clouds, vast amounts of energy are generated and released. Storms usually last one to two hours but the more severe ones can last much longer.

Storms are possibly the most dramatic of the common weather events. They can bring heavy rain, sometimes hail, thunder, lightning, and occasionally tornadoes or waterspouts, almost any of which can cause significant damage, particularly in urban areas. The starting point for any storm is differentially heated air. A typical summer thunderstorm occurs because the ground surface is heated locally to high temperatures, much higher than the surrounding air, as may happen after a period of very hot weather. The warm surface heats a "cell" of air which rises rapidly upwards (updrafts) to the troposphere creating turbulence. A large rising cell or bubble of air is formed, and clouds form as water vapor cools and condenses, forming ice crystals and water droplets. The clouds become electrically charged, both positively and negatively. As the air rises so cooler surrounding air descends (downdrafts) only to be heated again, so prolonging the life of the storm. The storm will continue as long as the cell of air remains warmer than the surrounding air.

LIGHTNING

Thunder and lightning are probably the most obvious and dramatic features of common storms. Although there is still no clear agreement on how lightning is formed it is believed that it is largely due to collisions between ice crystals. A huge electrical charge builds up as cloud particles become increasingly electrified and the charged particles separate. Positively charged particles develop at the top of the cloud whilst the base is negatively charged. The ground beneath the storm develops a positive "shadow." The electrical charge is discharged in a flash of lightning. A weak spark, the stepped leader, falls from the cloud and a positive leader rises from the ground. The return stroke, the main discharge from the ground to the cloud, moves along a channel created by the two leaders. Air around this channel is heated to about 54,000°F and the electrical discharge is about 1.5 million volts, mostly converted into heat energy.

A bolt of lightning is hotter than the surface of the sun. Typically a flash of lightning lasts only 0.2 seconds but generates enough heat to cause an isolated tree to explode as the water inside it is heated.

THUNDER AND LIGHTNING

The intense heat from a flash of lightning causes the air to expand and then contract violently, producing thunder.

Heated air expanding very rapidly creates sound waves—thunder. The speed of sound is much less than that of light so there are several seconds' delay between the flash of lightning and the sound of thunder. Lightning tends to strike at tall objects such as isolated trees or skyscrapers and, of course, lightning conductors. People who shelter beneath trees during a storm are often at severe risk of a lightning strike. Golfers are particularly prone and professional tournaments have a detailed weather forecast prepared for the duration as the consequences could be fatal. In a typical thunderstorm about 1000 lightning strikes take place each hour but a particularly severe thunderstorm in Quebec City, Canada, in July 1999, received the equivalent of 3000 an hour. It is not true that lightning never strikes twice: the Empire State Building in New York is hit about 100 times each year and was once famously hit 15 times in 15 minutes.

TYPES OF LIGHTNING

There are at least six different forms of lightning, each with its own individual characteristics and colors. Fork and sheet lightning are the most frequently seen. Sheet lightning can be seen when the lightning is close to the horizon and is in fact fork lightning within a cloud. The individual strikes can't be seen, but simply light up the distant cloud. Sheet lightning is the most common type of lightning. Fork lightning can be seen moving from cloud to ground, ground to cloud or cloud to cloud. Each fork of lightning is actually two strikes traveling quickly up and down the same path. The first bolt (the "leader stroke") zig-zags downward and completes the circuit between cloud and ground. This is followed a split second later by a huge surge (the "return stroke") that shoots back up the path just created. It is also the most destructive type of lightning as it often damages buildings and can kill.

Forked cloud-to-ground lightning over an urban area at night. Cloud-to-ground lightning occurs between a negatively charged cloud base and the positively charged ground. The other types of lightning are heat lightning, St Elmo's Fire, ball lightning and high altitude lightning—sometimes called red sprites, green elves or blue jets.

Above: A shelf cloud forms when rain-cooled air from a thunderstorm drops beneath the cloud and moves out from under it. This pushes warm air up over the top of the cloud, forming a leading edge that can run the whole length of a storm system.

Below: The intense heat from a flash of lightning causes the air to expand and then contract violently, producing thunder. The number of seconds between flash and thunder divided by three gives the approximate distance away of the lightning in kilometers and divided by five gives the approximate distance in miles.

Above: Thunderstorms occur in warm, humid conditions when dark cumulo-nimbus clouds build up in the sky.

Below: A supercell thunderstorm is a severe long-lived storm within which the wind speed and direction changes with height. This produces a strong rotating updraft of warm air, known as a mesocyclone, and a separate downdraft of cold air. Tornadoes may form in the mesocyclone, in which case the storm is classified as a tornadic supercell thunderstorm. The storms also produce torrential rain and hail.

HURRICANES

Hurricanes are storms that are formed
between the Tropics of Cancer and
Capricorn in the Atlantic and Pacific
Oceans as well as the Indian Ocean. They
have different names depending on where
they are formed. In the Atlantic they are
called hurricanes, in the north-west
Pacific, typhoons; in the Indian Ocean
they are known as tropical cyclones while
north of Australia they are sometimes
called Willy Willies! To form, hurricanes
need sea temperatures exceeding 81°F,
moisture and light winds above. The
hurricane season lasts from June 1 to
November 30 in the Atlantic and from
May 15 to November 30 in the Pacific.
Around 80 tropical storms form every
year with most in the south or south-east
of Asia. They are enormous features,
often between 120 and 430 miles in
diameter. They may last from a few days
to a week or more and their tracks are
notoriously unpredictable.

Palm trees being blown by violent winds.
A category 3 hurricane indicates winds between
110 mph and 130 mph.

HURRICANE FORMATION

August, 2005: Pedestrians battle against hurricane Katrina as it brings heavy storms to Fort Lauderdale, Florida, USA. Katrina did more damage further west, however, as the strongest part of the storm made landfall on the Gulf of Mexico coast. It devastated coastal regions of Mississippi and Louisiana. The poor and low-lying port city of New Orleans was left under polluted flood waters, and hundreds of people died.

The thick blanket of cloud which characterises the hurricane from space contains unrivaled quantities of water vapor and exceptionally heavy rainfall. At the center of the hurricane is the eye, an area of cloudless, calm weather which can be as much as 30 miles across. Here the air is descending and warming—meaning high pressure, calm weather and no clouds, a short respite before the remaining part of the hurricane continues on its course. As the strong winds approach land the final, deadly component begins to take shape—the storm surge. Low pressure in a hurricane has the effect of lifting the surface of the sea and the strong winds push the water ahead of it in huge waves. When they reach the coastline, the powerful waves crash ashore in surges. These can be up to 18 feet above normal sea level and may travel inland for many hundreds of feet where the coastline is low-lying, causing wide-spread flooding.

MEASURING HURRICANES

Type	Maximum Sustained Winds		Storm Surge		Damage Level
	KNOTS	MPH	Feet	Meters	
Depression	Less than 34	Less than 39	–	–	–
Tropical Storm	35–63	39-73	–	–	–
Category 1	64–82	74-95	3–5	1.0–1.7	minimal
Category 2	83–95	96–110	6–8	1.8–2.6	moderate
Category 3	96–113	111–130	9–12	2.7–3.8	extensive
Category 4	114–135	131–155	13–18	3.9–5.6	extreme
Category 5	136+	156+	19+	5.7+	catastrophic

Hurricanes are measured according to intensity, based on wind speed and storm surge severity, on the Saffir-Simpson scale. This ranges from 1 to 5, with 5 being the most severe and, if it makes landfall, with the most devastating consequences. At 5, wind speeds will be above 155 miles per hour and its storm surge will be over 18 ft above normal sea level. In the US the Atlantic is watched carefully by the National Oceanic and Atmospheric Administration (NOAA). All available technology is used—satellites, hurricane surveillance aircraft, radar, buoys, weather ships—to check for the formation of tropical storms; many lives and livelihoods depend on getting it right.

A hurricane is one of the most destructive forces of nature the Earth experiences. Once they reach land the energy source of the hurricane—warm seas—disappear, and it is downgraded to a tropical storm.

TRACKING HURRICANES

Eye of Hurricane Floyd as seen from the cockpit of a plane flown by the US Air Force Hurricane Hunters team. The Hercules plane is equipped to measure meteorological parameters, such as wind speed, humidity and atmospheric pressure. The data is then relayed to base, where computer models help predict the storm's future direction. These models have an accuracy of 70 percent, which allows authorities to implement damage limitation procedures such as evacuations.

Specialist national hurricane warning centers exist in many parts of the world to watch the oceans for any signs of tropical storm formation. Once the information is received, forecasts are made and the results are disseminated swiftly via a wide variety of media to all vulnerable communities and to ships at sea. Radio and television are used extensively but the internet is rapidly catching up as the preferred source of information. Telephone and SMS services are also widely used while ships at sea use fax and radio messages broadcast via satellites. For coastal communities in some countries, sirens are used to warn of the impending landfall of a hurricane, prompting evacuation and other precautionary measures to be taken. In the US the National Hurricane Center's website provides comprehensive advice and information for all in potentially vulnerable areas, from advance preparations such as securing homes to evacuation procedures.

NAMING HURRICANES

For hundreds of years, hurricanes that occurred in the West Indies were named after the Catholic saints' days on which they took place. During the late 19th and early 20th centuries, however, the Australian meteorologist Clement Wragge began to use the names of his friends, despised politicians, historical figures and mythological characters. Later storms were referred to by the coordinates of their latitudinal and longitudinal positions, but this method proved to be both slow and open to error, and so during World War II military meteorologists reverted to a system of naming. Using the convention of applying "she" to inanimate objects such as vehicles, hurricanes were given female names. The US army and navy then adopted a system of applying names from their joint phonetic alphabet, with the first hurricane being named "Able" in 1950. However, with the introduction of an international phonetic alphabet in 1953, that system was abandoned and female names were reintroduced by the US National Hurricane Center. In 1979, following claims of sexism, male names were introduced by the World Meteorological Organization, which continues to oversee the practice of hurricane naming.

Colored three-dimensional computer image, based on satellite data, of Hurricane Mitch. Today an alphabetical list of 21 names is used to name hurricanes (excluding the letters q, u, x, y, and z), alternating between male and female, and including English, French, and Spanish names, as these are the main languages used by the people who are most commonly affected by hurricanes.

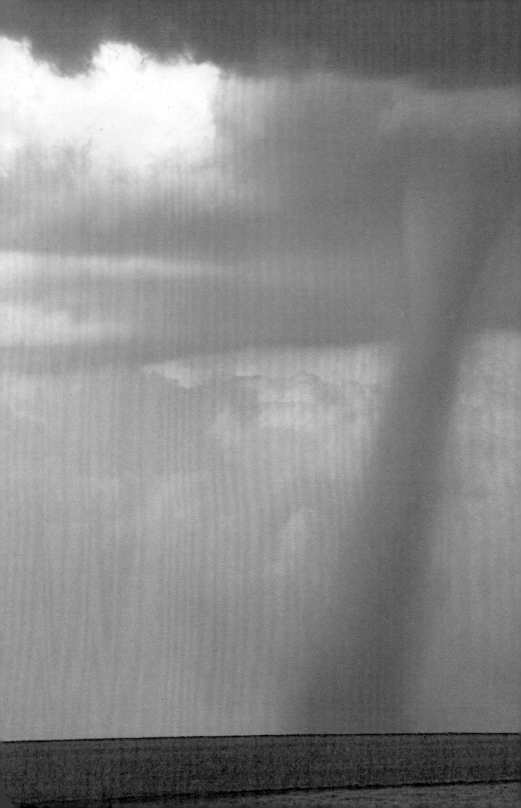

TORNADOES

A tornado is a rapidly spiraling column of air, usually associated with thunderstorms. They are generally small in scale, between a few feet to hundreds of feet across, and can last for only a few minutes or up to an hour, perhaps longer. Although the mechanisms responsible for their formation are by no means fully understood, tornadoes are likely to form when cold, dry air comes into contact with warm, moist air: this situation could occur along a cold front. Powerful thunderstorms can form along the front creating powerful updrafts. With height, the wind changes direction and the updraft of air begins to rotate, a process known as wind shear. The rotation extends downward and creates the recognizable funnel-like shape. If conditions are favorable the funnel reaches the ground and becomes a tornado. Very low pressure inside the column of air causes moisture to condense and makes it visible.

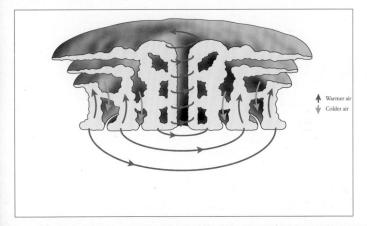

↑ Warmer air
↓ Colder air

Above: Diagram of a tornado. The characteristic feature of a tornado is the very powerful winds which spiral rapidly at speeds that can exceed 125 mph. Inside the column of air a powerful updraft causes very low pressure on the ground, while outside the column the winds rotate, anti-clockwise in the Northern Hemisphere, clockwise in the Southern.

Opposite: Most tornadoes occur in the United States, where the large land mass and great temperature contrasts between air masses favor their formation.

TORNADO ALLEY

The single most violent tornado in the USA took place in Oklahoma City in May 1999. Wind speeds during the tornado were the fastest ever recorded at 318 mph and resulted in 36 deaths with $1 billion worth of damage, making it the most costly in the state of Oklahoma.

The part of the USA which is most prone to damaging tornadoes is the mid-western states between the Rockies and the Appalachians, although tornadoes have been reported in every state. "Tornado Alley" is particularly vulnerable because it lies between the hot and humid air of the Gulf of Mexico and the cold and dry air from the Rockies. This leads to the formation of enormous cumulo-nimbus clouds, as much as 60,000 feet high. Sometimes these group together and form "supercells." The most dangerous tornadoes arise from these, along with thunderstorms and hail showers. In April 1974 just such conditions developed to create the country's largest tornado outbreak. In just 16 hours, 148 tornadoes hit 11 states killing 330 people and injuring more than 5300. Casualties would have been higher but for the tornado warning that was issued in advance.

MEASURING TORNADOES

F-Scale Number	Intensity	Wind Speed
F0	Gale tornado	64–116 kph (40–72 mph)
F1	Moderate tornado	117–180 kph (73–112 mph)
F2	Significant tornado	181–253 kph (113–157 mph)
F3	Severe tornado	254–332 kph (158–206 mph)
F4	Devastating tornado	333–418 kph (207–260 mph)
F5	Incredible tornado	Over 418 kph (260mph)

In the USA tornadoes are measured on the Fujita or F-scale which ranges from 0 to 5, whereas in the UK they are measured on the Torro or T-scale which ranges from 0 to 10. With both scales it is wind speed that is taken into consideration when calculating which level a tornado reaches. The most damaging tornado to affect the USA occurred in March 1925 in Tornado Alley. The towns of Murphysboro, Gorham and DeSoto were affected by the F5 tornado which caused 695 deaths and 2027 injuries. As a result of such events there has been considerable research into the meteorological conditions that cause tornadoes. Warning systems are in place via a wide range of media including, increasingly, the internet. Advice is available for organizations such as schools and hospitals, as well as for private individuals, on safety and construction of storm cellars.

A tornado is defined as a localized and violently destructive windstorm occuring over land, characterized by a funnel-shaped cloud extending towards the ground.

STORM CHASERS

Most storm-chasing takes place on the Great Plains of North America, but there are also groups and individuals dedicated to the pursuit in Australia, Israel, and much of Europe. Such is their success at tracking tornadoes that it is now possible for the adventurous to take a holiday with storm-chasing organizations in the USA.

It is difficult to predict when a tornado will occur since no one is absolutely certain how they form. What is predictable, however, is that, if conditions are right, they can form almost anywhere. National weather services monitor the situations in which tornadoes may form in order to be able to give tornado watch warnings to the media. Meteorological offices use the most up-to-date technology to assist them, including radar and satellite data. Despite that, intrepid scientists willingly track weather systems likely to produce tornadoes using specially adapted vehicles. Storm chasers are involved in the tracking of tornadoes, collecting valuable data as they do so and offering advice on protection from the effects. Their work has provided another set of invaluable data to aid the prediction of tornadoes and to provide more accurate warnings.

WATERSPOUTS

Waterspouts are far more common than many people expect and frequently pose a hazard to those in small craft at sea. Two types of waterspouts form, the more dangerous of which is the tornadic waterspout. These often begin overland as conventional tornadoes and drift out to sea. They are very different in formation to the second type, the fair-weather waterspout. These are more common and are similar to the "dust devils" or swirls of dust that are sometimes seen on hot days over land in the summer. They form over open sea or large lakes in the late summer or early fall when the water temperature is at its highest. If a cool air mass then blows over the warm water the air becomes humid which causes strong convection currents to form. If these are sufficiently strong, waterspouts may develop.

Giant waterspout seen in the Bermuda Triangle area. A waterspout is a funnel-shaped mass of cloud and water, similar to a tornado occurring at sea. It is more a feature of tropical and subtropical waters than of higher latitude seas. An inverted cone-shape cloud descends from a cumulonimbus cloud until it reaches a cone of spray rising from the sea. A column of water is formed between sea and cloud. The spout may be several hundred feet high and can last for half an hour.

AVALANCHES

Avalanches are seasonal hazards which occur when a large amount of snow (or rock) slides down a mountainside. When snowfall is heavy and a significant build-up occurs, an avalanche is likely. Anything more than a gentle wind can contribute to the build-up of snow on downwind slopes. Heavy snowfall makes the snow on the slope unstable, partly because of the extra weight and partly because the snow has not had time to bond; the first 24 hours after a storm are the most critical. Rain can also contribute as it adds extra weight and may help lubricate the snow in the lower layers. In addition, the steeper the slope, the greater the likelihood of an avalanche occurring. Slope aspect may also contribute to the risk of an avalanche as a southerly aspect will be warmer.

In February 1999 in Galtuer, Austria a series of massive avalanches killed 38 people. Heavy snowfall—up to 16 inches in one day—was made unstable by strong winds. At the end of the year, the same region was hit by yet more avalanches which killed a further 15. Between 1998 and the start of 2000, Austria recorded 56 occurences in which 50 people were killed and a further 70 were injured. Austria and the other Alpine countries of France, Switzerland, and Italy are those which are hit most frequently by avalanches, but the events of 1999 were nevertheless highly unusual.

Avalanches occur when large amounts of snow and ice become loose and flow down a mountain under the force of gravity. They can be extremely destructive. As well as the force of snow and ice themselves, the wave of air in front of the rapidly moving snow can cause buildings to explode before the avalanche hits them.

BLIZZARDS

The worst ice storm to affect the Great Lakes area of the USA and Canada took place over a few days in early January 1998. The Canadian side of the border experienced 80 hours of freezing rain, twice as much as the annual average. This led to 28 deaths, mainly from hypothermia, 945 injuries and 4 million homes left without power, forcing 600,000 people to leave their homes in Ontario, Quebec and New Brunswick.

Winter storms create difficult conditions for everyone who experiences them. In 1993 a massive storm dropped snow in blizzard conditions which affected half the population of the USA over 26 states as well as southern parts of Canada and even as far south as Mexico: 270 people died and a further 48 were missing at sea. Snow as lay as deep as 15 feet and up to 50 feet fell, including as much snow as normally falls in Alabama in an entire winter. No wonder it was called the storm of the century. Different definitions of a blizzard exist, but one in common use states that visibility must be down to 0.25 mile for at least four consecutive hours, must include snow or ice as precipitation and wind speeds of at least 35 mph—7 on the Beaufort Scale. Blizzards can occur when polar cyclones develop.

HAILSTORMS

In May 2000 the worst hailstorm in over 30 years struck parts of Illinois in the USA. During the storm hail ranging from golf ball to tennis ball in size fell. Around 100,000 homes lost power, train services were disrupted and over 100 flights were canceled. At its worst, the hail was over 3 inches deep. On another occasion in Hainan province, China, 25 people died and hundreds were injured during a severe hailstorm.

Hailstorms of this magnitude are relatively rare occurrences but the sight of smaller, less damaging hail is much more common. Hailstones are usually only a fraction of an inch in diameter but can sometimes grow to as much as 6 inches and weigh more than 1lb. Hail of pea or golf ball size is not uncommon in severe storms.

View of a cumulo-nimbus hail storm cloud in in the Black Rock Desert, Nevada. The hail forms in cumulo-nimbus clouds due to the presence of violent convection currents. Some hailstones can be over 4 inches across, and cause severe damage to property and crops.

MONSOONS

We tend to assume that the monsoon is a regular, reliable source of rainfall but this is not always the case. If the rainfall is late or less than expected it can lead to crop failure and starvation. In India, a country where the population is already 1 billion and is predicted to exceed 1.4 billion by 2025, the rainfall is vital and even minor variations can be catastrophic. It is the rainfall that is most striking but this sometimes has unwanted side effects of flooding. This is short-term but nonetheless is highly disruptive, causing immense damage and financial loss to countries that find it difficult to cope at the best of times.

Modern forecasting methods allow governments to plan for the onset of the monsoon to reduce these effects. It is now possible to predict the arrival of the monsoon to within two or three days.

Over half of the world's population relies on the rains brought by the monsoon rains of Asia, Africa and Australia. It is the so-called "monsoon subcontinent" of south and south-east Asia—India, Pakistan, and Bangladesh—that we tend to associate most with this rainfall phenomenon. More than 75 percent of India's annual rainfall occurs during the monsoon. During the Northern Hemisphere winter the high pressure system over Siberia intensifies, causing strong north-easterly winds which blow towards the Equator. They remain dry until they blow across the South China Sea and then become the north-easrly monsoon of south-east

Asia. The intense low that forms over central Asia draws in the south-easterly trade winds that deflect toward the south-west as they cross the Equator. This is responsible for the heavy rainfall over southern Asia.

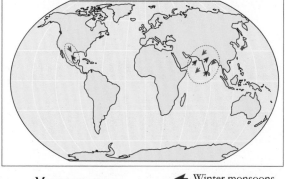

Monsoon areas

← Winter monsoons
➤ Summer monsoons

Monsoon flooding on the plains of India, showing half-submerged field systems. Monsoon winds blow in India from June to mid-December, but some years they arrive weeks late, and occasionally fail to appear at all. Asia has the most pronounced monsoon conditions— particularly in India, Bangladesh, Burma, Thailand, and the Philippines.

FLOODING

Typical flood defences include "soft engineering" schemes such as earth embankments and tree planting or more costly "hard engineering" such as dams and flood barriers for example the Thames Flood Barrier—seen here with the gates closed. The gates are shut when there is a high risk of tidal flooding, or for maintenance. Closing the barrier seals off part of the upper Thames with a continuous steel wall spanning 1700 feet across the river.

There are, broadly speaking, two types of flood—the river or mainstream flood and the flash flood. The river or mainstream flood is usually caused by heavy rainfall over an extended period of time. In contrast, a flash flood is usually caused by a short period of intense rainfall. About 40 percent of all casualties in natural disasters occur in floods: in the USA floods are the second biggest killer, responsible for an average of 84 deaths between 1984 and 2003. In only 6 inches of fast flowing water a person can be knocked off his or her feet and in similar conditions with 2 feet of water it is possible to see cars washed away. Flooding is sometimes worse in urban areas where summer thunderstorms are common and the ground is tarmac. This material is impermeable and so cannot absorb the extra water which has to run off the surface. Urban areas are deliberately designed to ensure water is drained away swiftly into rivers and this inevitably increases the flood risk.

GREAT MISSISSIPPI FLOOD

Flooding is, of course, a natural event on rivers. The annual flooding of the Nile was a critical part of the way people used the land as it provided the silt which created the natural fertility of the soils that the population depended upon. The Mississippi in the USA also regularly flooded but this was never really a problem until human settlement along the flood plain developed from the late 19th century. Today huge sums of money are spent on protecting, not always successfully, the settlements that have grown up there from the risk of flooding.

The Mississippi, one of the longest rivers in the United States, flows over 2300 miles north to south across the USA. It has the third largest drainage basin in the world, and heavy rainfall can cause massive flooding further downstream and kill large numbers of livestock.

Some of the worst floods in America have occurred on the Mississippi River, including the Great Mississippi Flood of 1927.

FLOODS IN BANGLADESH

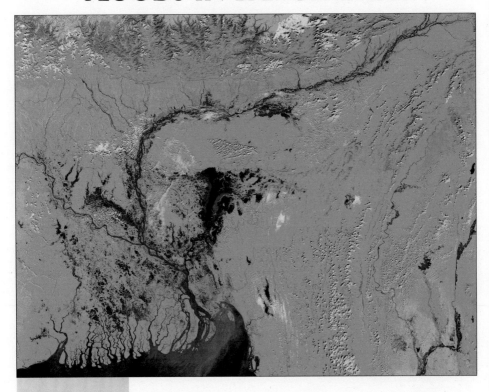

False-color satellite image of floods caused by monsoon rains in Bangladesh (center left) and India (far left, center right). Rivers have burst their banks and the terrain surrounding the Ganges River (center left) and Brahmaputra River (upper right) is waterlogged. Standing water is visible, particularly in Dhaka (center), the capital city of Bangladesh.

Perhaps the area most associated with serious flooding is the small country of Bangladesh in Asia. Its physical geography lies at the heart of the causes of flooding in the region. Bangladesh is situated at the head of the Bay of Bengal where it narrows as it reaches the Ganges Delta. To the north lies the Himalaya range with its permanent ice and snow fields. Some 150 rivers criss-cross the country. Over 50 percent of the country is less than 16 feet above sea level and is affected every year by torrential rain from the annual monsoon. With a population of 160 million, Bangladesh is one of the world's most densely populated countries and also one of the poorest. Many people live in the delta region which naturally floods, causing the position of the innumerable islands and distributaries it comprises to change. The annual floods provide the water required for irrigation of crops such as rice and millet and add fertile silt to the soil bringing important benefits to the region.

FLOODS IN EUROPE

The summer of 2002 saw widespread flooding over much of central and western Europe. The city that was perhaps most badly affected was the Czech capital, Prague. In August of that year, heavy rain fell from a slow-moving frontal system which had also affected much of the rest of Europe. The river Vltava rose ominously, forcing the country's president to enforce an evacuation of 40,000 people. Despite this, the flood defences were breached, leading to transport links being cut and causing significant damage to the city's architectural wonders. Many other towns and cities in the country were equally badly disrupted as rivers flooded, leading to 10 deaths and hundreds of thousands of people being made homeless. At the same time, in Austria and Romania, the worst floods for a century claimed a similar number of deaths. However, it was in the Black Sea area of Russia that most lives were lost: here 58 people died and over 1500 were evacuated as the floodwaters flowed down the Danube.

In Europe, floods are the most common natural disasters. Between 1975 and 2001, 238 major floods were recorded in the region. Since 1990 about 2000 people have died and some 400,000 have been left homeless.

FLASH FLOODING

Flash floods are by their very nature unpredictable and potentially deadly. A flash flood occurs within a few hours of the rainfall event. The rainfall is usually a very intense and short burst of rain over a relatively small area after a heavy storm such as a summer thunderstorm. Humid air will rise quickly and if it remains relatively stationary it will drop all its rain over a small area of land. If humid air rises over mountains and is kept in a small area by the wind it will also drop most of its rain over the hills, forcing it to flow down hillsides into the valley below. When the ground is baked hard by the sun any rain that falls will not be absorbed by the earth. Instead it will be forced to run off over the surface and make its way into rivers and canyons. Water in flash floods often moves at incredible speeds catching people unawares and can also lead to mudslides.

An example of a flash flood also occurred in the USA in June 1990 in Shadyside, Ohio. Here 4 inches of rain fell in less than 2 hours creating a 30 feet high wall of water which then flowed through parts of the town. Twenty-six people died and it was estimated that between $6 and 8 million worth of damage was caused.

The Bisagno River rages under a bridge in Genoa, Italy after a flash flood.

DROUGHT

Aral Sea boat stranded amongst dunes. The Aral Sea, inland between Kazakhstan and Uzbekistan, was supplied by rivers, but in the 1930s these were diverted to irrigate crops, notably cotton. As less water flowed to the sea, it began shrinking through evaporation. It has halved in area since the 1960s, and its salinity has increased dramatically, leaving ghost towns that were once thriving fishing communities, and damaging the ecosystem.

Although there are over 100 different definitions, a drought may be best defined as a period of time when there is significantly less rainfall than normal. Being more precise than that is difficult; in the USA a drought is a period of a month or more with less than 30 percent of normal rainfall but in the UK it is possible to experience a drought when a period of only three weeks of no rainfall occurs. In some countries drought is a way of life, a commonly occurring event which the population living in the area have learned to manage over the centuries. For others, periodic droughts cause chaos. The effects can be devastating, with failed crops causing significant economic difficulties that cost billions of pounds, even famine, deaths, and malnutrition-related disease. The impact on the natural environment is equally devastating with soil erosion, and loss of native vegetation and animal habitats. Frequent, persistent drought can lead to the ideal conditions for bush fires and dust storms.

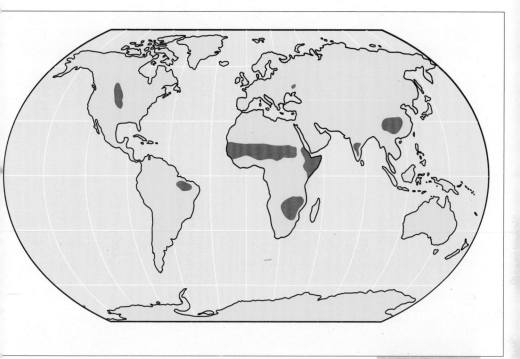

The Sahel region south of the Sahara Desert in Africa normally
has unreliable rainfall which can be managed by the small
native population who have adopted management strategies
over the centuries. When this turned into a long-term drought
during the 1970s and 1980s, however, the effects in countries
such as Ethiopia and Kenya were catastrophic. Deaths ran into
the thousands and many tens of thousands were temporarily or
permanently displaced. In the 1930s the great Dust Bowl
drought severely affected much of the USA—some regions
experienced eight years of continuous drought. The lack of rain
was exacerbated by the poor agricultural practices of the time.
The grasslands of the Great Plains had been deeply plowed
and, when rainfall was sufficient, produced good yields of
cereals. Once the drought really hit, however, nothing would
grow and the soil was left bare and exposed to the wind. Many
farmers had to leave their farms and seek a new life elsewhere.
The effects of this drought led to profound political and social
changes as well as significant environmental damage.

Areas at risk of
drought, which
is classed as
significantly less
rainfall than
normal. In some
countries,
drought is a way
of life and their
populations have
learned to adapt,
but prolonged or
unexpected
drought can
cause chaos.

BUSH FIRES

Smoke rising from the flames of a bush fire in California, USA. Most fires are the result of drought and lightning strikes. However, they are increasingly caused by human activity, whether deliberate burnoffs, unextinguished campfires or discarded cigarette butts. Small blazes can get out of hand very quickly and turn into raging infernos.

These are a natural phenomena that are most common in Australia but which occur wherever there is wood, leaves, and scrubby vegetation that can burn. The causes are most commonly associated with drought and lightning strikes and sometimes human action. Where the climate is moist enough to allow vegetation growth but has hot and dry periods which allow for dried-out branches and leaves, there is the potential for fire. This material is highly flammable so following a drought, and when the winds are strong, the smallest spark can ignite a fire which can spread rapidly through an area. Fires are inevitably more common in summer where the conditions are right. The old wood, sometimes called "slash," which has fallen to the ground is ideal fuel. In Los Alerces National Park, Argentina, this slash is routinely cleared from the areas where humans visit because the high risk of lightning strikes can lead to huge fires.

DUST STORMS

Dust or sand storms are common occurrences in arid or semi-arid areas of the world such as deserts. When the land is heated by intense solar radiation, convection takes place; in other words the air rises, creating an area of low pressure. It is replaced by cooler air rushing in from an area of higher pressure, this is wind. The inrush of wind can be fast enough to move sand dunes in desert areas like the Sahara and can create problems for travel, often obscuring roads and creating very low visibility conditions. If the topsoil is light and uncultivated the wind may blow it away and deposit it where it is not wanted, creating a nuisance. Dust and sand storms can move material many thousands of miles. At times the leading edge of a sand or dust storm may appear as a solid wall and reach as high as 5000 feet.

Sahara Desert in Chad seen from space. A sandstorm is seen at upper center (white) over the Djourab region. The winds in this region blow predominantly toward the south-west, toward the horizon in this image. They are channeled between two highland areas (dark), the Tibesti Mountains (center right) and the Ennedi Massif (center left). These winds have created large streak features on the plains. The Tibesti Mountains are the highest point in the Sahara Desert.

VOLCANIC EFFECTS ON THE WEATHER

Volcanic eruptions have a pronounced impact on the weather. The eruption of the Indonesian volcano, Tamboro, in 1815 caused a dismal summer across the world the following year. During the eruption huge quantities of dust, ash, and gas were ejected into the atmosphere. These elements, such as sulfur dioxide droplets, combined to reflect incoming solar radiation back into the atmosphere and so reduce the temperature at the Earth's surface by as much as 5°F. It was a time of major weather-related disruption recorded in western Europe and northern USA. In New England and Canada each of the summer months of 1816 witnessed frosts. In addition the aerosols given off were responsible for the brilliant sunsets witnessed around the world for several years afterwards.

In Iceland, the Laki volcanic eruption of 1783 was one of the largest effusive (lava) eruptions of historical times. It was this eruption that prompted the American diplomat—scientist, Benjamin Franklin, to hypothesise that there was a link between volcanic emissions and a reduction in temperatures. More recently when Mount Pinatubo in the Philippines erupted in 1991 it ejected enormous quantities of sulfur dioxide—an estimated 24 US tons—into the stratosphere where it combined with water vapor to form an aerosol of sulfuric acid. This blocked out the sun's rays sufficiently to cause global temperatures to cool by as much as 0.5°C during the following year.

As recently as the 1980s it was discovered that the Yellowstone area of the USA is a so-called "super-volcano," a volcano of such an enormous size that when it erupts its effects are likely to be catastrophic, not just in the USA itself. It has been estimated that a future eruption, given the amount of dust and gases emitted, would have the effect of lowering global temperatures by 9°F, would cause widespread famine and possibly precipitate another ice age.

The big island of Hawaii is entirely formed by volcanic activity. Volcanic eruptions can send vast amounts of ash and sulfur dioxide into the upper atmosphere. The sulfur dioxide reacts with stratospheric water vapor to produce a dense haze that can stay in the stratosphere for years. This haze absorbs some incoming solar radiation and reflects more back out to space. This raises the temperature of the stratosphere and cools the lower levels of the troposphere.

Unusual
Weather Opticals

THE SPECTRUM OF LIGHT

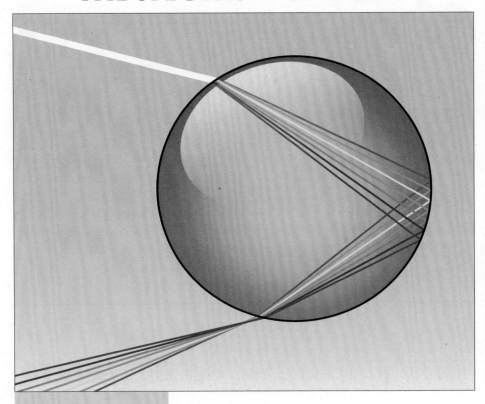

Light separates into its component colors as it travels at different speeds. Sunlight is made up of colors that the eye can see. When combined, these colors appear white, a principle first demonstrated by Newton in 1666. As light moves through air of different densities it refracts. This disperses the light into its different component colors.

There can be few people who do not recall learning the colors of the rainbow when in school, but how many of us can remember exactly why there are these colors and why a rainbow exists at all? Sunlight consists of a mixture of colors from across the spectrum. We can see this most clearly when sunlight shines through a prism. Light separates into its component colors as it travels at different speeds through the prism, a process known as refraction. This optical phenomenon is also seen to occur naturally and is responsible for some of the most unusual optical events connected with weather.

OPTICAL EFFECTS

These effects include the rainbow, of course, but also the famous mirages, coronas, and the spectacular light show of the high latitudes, the auroras. The latter, either the Aurora Borealis in the Northern Hemisphere or its southern relative the Aurora Australis, are sometimes better known as the Northern and Southern Lights respectively. Once seen, the rapidly changing colored lights that illuminate the night sky are impossible to forget. Perhaps the most famous optical illusion formed by the sun's rays is the mirage. Countless images in cartoon, literature, and film highlight this illusory phenomenon. The less well known corona is formed around the sun or the moon by, once again, light refracting as it passes through the atmosphere.

A rainbow is the resulting optical effect of sunlight passing through water vapor. The light traveling at different speeds through the vapor is refracted into its component colors.

RAINBOWS

A rainbow is formed by the way the light bends as it passes through the atmosphere. A rainbow is sunlight spread out into its spectrum of colors and refracted by water droplets in the Earth's atmosphere. As it is seen as an arc in the sky it lends its name to the bow part of rainbow. Some of the light that has entered the water droplet is reflected, allowing the viewer to see the different colors, but only if the viewer is standing with his back to the sun.

The traditional view of a rainbow is that it is made up of seven colors—red, orange, yellow, green, blue, indigo, and violet—but in fact it is a continuum of colors from red to violet.

Rainbows occur when the observer is facing falling rain and with the Sun behind them. White light is reflected inside the raindrops and split into its component colors by refraction. The second, fainter rainbow is caused by different raindrops, which are higher in the atmosphere. These raindrops reflect the sunlight twice, causing the order of the second rainbow's colors to reverse.

HALOES, SUNDOGS AND CORONAS

For many centuries traditional weather forecasters have used the occurrence of haloes as an indicator of imminent rain, but what is a halo? Airborne ice crystals sometimes act as prisms and when sun—or moon-light passes through the crystals they refract, that is bend, slightly. As many of the ice crystals may be in random patterns, circular haloes result. The most common angle of refraction is 22° and most haloes are produced in this way. At certain points on the halo particularly bright patches form. These are known as sundogs, sometimes parhelia, or mock suns. Haloes and sundogs occur frequently in Polar regions but can also be seen in lower latitudes. As the refraction of light is also dependent on color, haloes and sundogs exhibit considerable variation in coloring. Haloes do sometimes precede rain, as the ice crystals responsible for them becoming visible are seen in cirrus clouds which sometimes precede a frontal system that brings rain.

A corona is a feature which is produced when light is diffracted by small particles, the light passes around the tiny spherical droplets. The result is a pattern of lightly colored rainbow-like bands that surround the sun or the moon when viewed through alto-cumulus clouds. It is best seen around the moon as it is less bright than the sun (and safer to look at) so does not swamp the effect.

Lunar corona, seen through cirriform clouds. A corona is the diffraction of light as it passes through water droplets in clouds. The cirriform clouds are possibly thin high-level cirrostratus nebulosis clouds. The size and regularity of the water droplets dictates the size and color of the corona.

AURORAE

Famously seen in the night skies of the higher latitudes is the Aurora Borealis or its cousin in the Southern Jemisphere the Aurora Australis. They appear as rapidly moving differently colored areas of light in the night sky. Aurorae occur when particles from the sun interact with the Earth's atmosphere. The particles are called a "solar wind," which is linked to an 11 year solar sunspot cycle, and solar flares. These are quickly moving charged particles emitted from the sun. The Polar regions are the only ones not protected from these particles by the Earth's magnetic field and so it is only at the poles that the solar wind can interact with the Earth's atmosphere.

When the charged particles collide with the Earth's air molecules energy is emitted as light. This is seen only at or close to the Poles in a ring called an "aurora oval." When there are more particles during a great deal of activity when there are many solar flares—the ring expands and the lights are seen further south or north. They occur very high in the atmosphere—40 miles above airplanes but can occur up to 600 miles above the Earth which is higher than space shuttles fly.

Aurora Borealis or Northern Lights display over silhouetted conifer trees in Finland in early October. In the Northern Hemisphere the Aurora Borealis, is named after the Roman goddess of the dawn, Aurora, and the Greek name for the north wind, Boreas. The Aurora Borealis most often occurs from September to October, and from March to April.

MIRAGE

How many movies of a particular genre made during the 20th century have shown someone in the desert struggling with his thirst have an image appear before him of a source of water only for it on closer inspection to turn out to be a mirage? This idea of a mirage appearing only when someone struggles with heat stroke is erroneous. A mirage is not a mere illusion—it can be photographed—but it is unlikely to be as near and so not as tangible as the viewer may hope. A mirage is an atmospheric phenomenon caused by the differential heating of layers of air. As air warms up, it expands, and this affects its refractive index. Light rays slanting down from a cool layer of air to a hot layer (such as one in contact with hot ground) will be be refracted to a shallower angle. If the angle is sufficiently shallow, the light rays are refracted so that they appear to be reflected upward. Therefore a mirage gives an image of the sky and any scenery behind it.

There are two main types of mirage—inferior and superior— both of which are caused by the refraction of light passing through the atmosphere. An inferior mirage is seen below an object such as the sky or the sun, whereas a superior mirage is seen above it. A commonly seen example of an inferior mirage is the shimmering pool of water often seen on roads on a hot day. The refraction of the light is caused by the very large temperature differences which develop close to the road surface. The light bends so much that an image of the sky shows on the road. The less common superior mirage often shows itself in the form of the setting or rising sun. It is in fact a mirage of the actual sun which is in reality below the horizon. It is caused by a layer of warmer air above a colder one—a temperature inversion. If the temperature difference is great enough the warmer air refracts the light.

Desert Mirage photographed in the Western Desert, Egypt. A large mirage glimmers in the heat of the desert sun, casting reflections of the mountains beyond it. When light passes through different mediums its speed changes, which leads to the light bending or refracting. This can happen in air of different densities such as when the temperature changes.

HISTORY AND CULTURE

WEATHER FOLKLORE

One of the most well-known weather lore proverbs—"Red sky at night, shepherd's delight; red sky in morning, shepherd's warning," has a basis in truth. A red sunset often occurs as the result of light being filtered by an approaching high pressure system from the west, which tends to bring fair weather; whilst a red sunrise in the east often indicates that such a system has passed over, and a low pressure system, which is often accompanied by unsettled weather, may be following behind.

Today, meteorologists have an impressive array of technological devices and scientific techniques at their disposal, in order to forecast or predict changing patterns of weather and climate. However, for thousands of years, man relied upon a combination of superstition and observation; over time ideas that particular gods controlled various aspects of the weather were gradually complemented and superseded by looking at natural indicators such as wind direction, cloud formations, the color of the sky, and certain optical effects, and also the behavior of animals and plants. The ability to predict the weather was of chief importance to people such as farmers, sailors, fishermen, and shepherds, as well as others who lived off the land and the sea, and whose livelihoods often depended upon weather conditions, but across the globe almost every culture developed its own weather lore, which often found expression in proverbs and rhymes.

ANCIENT BELIEFS

Many people will know that Ra is the ancient Egyptian sun god, but he is only one of many dozens of others found in different cultures at different historical periods. In an attempt to understand nature and the weather in particular, many ancient peoples devised "weather gods" who controlled the wind, sun, and rain and who shaped the harvests and the availability of wild animals for food. Early people were superstitious and fearful but believed that gods would be appeased by offerings and rituals. Many cultures had gods of wind such as Aeolus in ancient Greece and Fujin a Japanese Shinto demon. The Japanese World War Two "Kamikaze" (divine wind) pilots took their name from the name of a god of storms and winds. Zeus (Greek), Raiden (Japan) and Indra (Hindu) were all gods associated with thunder and, particularly, lightning. The vital life-giving sun was worshiped by many cultures including the Egyptians and the Incas with Inti, who was personified as a golden disk with a human face, whilst Ra was depicted as traveling across the sky in a sun boat each day.

It is believed that human sacrifices were made to the Aztec rain and harvest god Tialoc whereas Quetzalcoatl (pictured above) was believed to be the creator of life and in control of the vital rain-bearing winds. Quetzalcoatl was a Toltec and Aztec god who represented the forces of nature. Quetzalcoatl also became a representation of the rain, the celestial waters and their associated winds.

THE RENAISSANCE AND EARLY SCIENCE

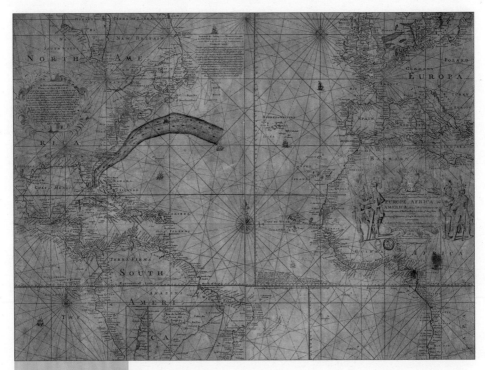

During the 15th century the expansion of trade routes led to a greater understanding of the Earth and the weather. Magellan, Columbus and other explorers of the period began to recognize the pattern of winds across the oceans and kept records of the weather. The Earth had been circumnavigated twice by 1600.

Greek scholar Aristotle's book *Meteorologica* was perhaps the first scientific attempt to understand the weather. Very early scientific attempts to explain the weather were carried out by Theophrastus, a student of Aristotle, who wrote *On Weather Signs*. Meteorology did not progress in Europe until the Renaissance period in the 15th century. During this time new and improved scientific instruments for measuring and understanding the weather were developed. Significant figures of the time include Galileo Galilei (1564–1642), Leonardo daVinci (1452–1519) and Evangelista Torricelli (1608–47). Galileo is perhaps most famous in this context for the invention of a thermometer and was convinced that many weather phenomena could be explained by scientific means. daVinci pioneered the study of atmospheric optics and was responsible for encouraging an interest in understanding the forces of nature.

THE AGE OF REASON

Pascal, Newton, and Celsius are all names we associate with different important scientific and meteorological discoveries during the 17th and 18th centuries. The French scientist Blaise Pascal discovered that air pressure changed with height and realized that air pressure was related to changes in the weather. In England, Isaac Newton devised laws of physics that remain the basis of today's weather forecasting computer models. A German physicist, Gabriel Fahrenheit developed the eponymous temperature scale in 1724. Fahrenheit dedicated much of his time to developing meteorological instruments, including reliable alcohol and mercury-based thermometers, which he produced commercially from around 1717 until 1736, the year of his death. During this period the wealthy and educated were able to take advantage of the newly developing weather recording instruments to make their own observations. One pioneering American philosopher-statesman, Benjamin Franklin conducted a landmark—and highly dangerous— experiment in 1752 to see if lightning was in fact an electrical discharge. He is also believed to be the inventor of the lightning rod which protects buildings from direct strikes.

Illustration of Benjamin Franklin and his son William, performing their famous experiment on June 15, 1752, flying a kite in a thunderstorm. A metal wire on the kite attracted a lightning strike and electricity flowed down the string to a key, charging a Leyden jar (capacitor) seen near Franklin's hand. This experiment proved that lightning was an electrical phenomenon, and supported Franklin's invention of lightning rods. Some scientists died repeating the experiment, and the Franklins were lucky they were not killed themselves.

WEATHER AND WAR

The course of history has been altered by the vagaries of the weather. Throughout history, there are numerous similar examples of the weather's effect on the outcome of military campaigns. Julius Caesar invaded Britain in 54 BC, but this was not his first attempt to conquer the British Isles. In 55 BC his navy was thwarted by the strong north-westerly winds which made crossing the English Channel impossible. A later invasion of Britain, this time by the Spanish Armada in the 16th century, was also affected by the weather. In the late summer of 1588 the Spanish ships retreated after defeat by Francis Drake's naval forces. A deep depression, bringing strong winds and very high seas in the north of Scotland and Ireland wrecked the remaining Armada, drowning many hundreds of men.

During the mid-17th century in northern Europe, when Denmark attacked Sweden, severe winter weather enabled the Swedish forces to cross the frozen ice from Jutland to Zealand, forcing the Danes to surrender. In 1812, Napoleon's Grand Army was forced to retreat from Russia, partly on account of the severe winter weather. Only two years later, at the Battle of Waterloo, thunderstorms, accompanied by torrential rains, forced Napoleon to delay his attack on the British, which enabled Prussian forces to join them, whilst the French advance was slowed considerably, and the battlefield turned into a quagmire.

The weather was also a significant player during World War II. Calm weather was vital for the D-Day landings in June 1944, and forecasters were central to the invasion plans. Weather also played a crucial role on the Eastern front; the Germans were so confident of a quick victory, that they had not prepared for the severe Russian winter. As Germany tried desperately to provide winter clothing for its troops, the Russians were able to regroup and begin their counter-offensive.

A lithograph depicting Napoleon's return from Moscow, after an original painting by Jan Chelminski. The Russian winter combined with disease, desertions, and casualties sustained in various minor actions caused thousands of losses in the French camp.

WEATHER IN ART

The weather and its elements have featured in artistic representations for thousands of years; even being known from prehistoric pictographs and petroglyphs, which were painted and carved in caves and on other rock faces. From these earliest depictions, there subsequently developed a long tradition of representing the natural world and its weather, particularly in sky and landscape painting, which continues to this day. However, today there are also artists who incorporate natural weather phenomena into their art, replicate them artificially, or use meteorological data to produce their works. It is thought that realistic painting of the sky began with the ancient Greeks and was continued by the Romans, but it also features prominently in ancient Oriental paintings. The first major explosion of weather in art, however, resulted from the increased interest in observing nature that was introduced during the Renaissance of the 15th and 16th centuries, with artists such as Leonardo daVinci, Rembrandt, Titian, Albrecht Dürer, Jan van Eyck, and both Brueghels, all noted for their rendering of clouds and skies.

Later, during the 18th and 19th centuries, the weather became a major concern of the Romantic artists in western Europe, many of whom produced symbolic, but naturalistic depictions of the landscape. The effects and changing qualties of sunlight was central to the French Impressionist movement, which emphasized the technique of painting outdoors amongst the elements.

"Hunters in the Snow" (1565) by Pieter the Elder Brueghel. Brueghel was a Flemish Renaissance painter known for his landscapes and peasant scenes. He is often credited as being the first western painter to paint landscapes for their own sake, rather than as a backdrop to a religious allegory. His winter landscapes of 1565 are corroborative evidence of the severity of winters during the "Little Ice Age."

WEATHER IN LITERATURE

Scene from *The Tempest*. Shakespeare's play opens with Prospero, rightful Duke of Milan, raising a storm in order to run his brother Alonso's ship aground. In this play, the power of nature and the weather over humans can be seen as a major theme.

From ancient scriptures to modern novels, the weather has been a recurrent subject in a great deal of literature throughout the ages. It is frequently employed in fiction, not only observationally or as a simple aesthetic aside, but as a device for setting tone and emotional atmosphere; it may not only inform the plot of a story, but actually drive and parallel it. In the dramatic works of Shakespeare the weather is frequently an integral element, and it was often employed symbolically. For example, he often used stormy weather as a metaphor for the difficulties of human relationships, or to parallel violent events, as in the tragedies Macbeth and King Lear. In the late18th and early 19th centuries poets such as Wordsworth and Keats, formed the nucleus of the Romantic movement in England which had counterparts elsewhere. Weather featured in many of their best-known poems such as "I Wandered Lonely as a Cloud," by Wordsworth and "To Autumn," by Keats.

THE CELSIUS SCALE

The Celsius scale was originally created in 1742 by the Swedish astronomer Anders Celsius, taking zero as the boiling point of water, which, he accurately demonstrated, varied according to atmospheric pressure, and 100 degrees as the melting point of ice, which did not. Two years later in 1744, the same year that Celsius died, the scientist Carolus Linnaeus is thought to have then reversed Celsius's scale, so that zero degrees represented the melting point of ice, and 100 degrees denoted the boiling point of water. Today, it is the reversed Celsius scale that persists, and which is used throughout the scientific community worldwide. It has also become generally accepted for non-scientific purposes, having been introduced as part of the international metrication process of the 1960s and 1970s. Since 1954 however, the Celsius scale has been related to the Kelvin scale within the scientific world, with "absolute zero" and the "triple point" of scientifically standardized water replacing the melting point of ice and the boiling point of water.

Illustration of a weather station at the Greenwich Royal Observatory, London in 1880. The station contained an automatic anemometer, which measured the direction and strength of the wind. The science of meteorology advanced greatly during the late 19th century due to the development of telegraphy. This allowed data to be quickly collected from many weather stations at once. The first daily weather maps were published in 1860.

THE MARINERS' INFLUENCE

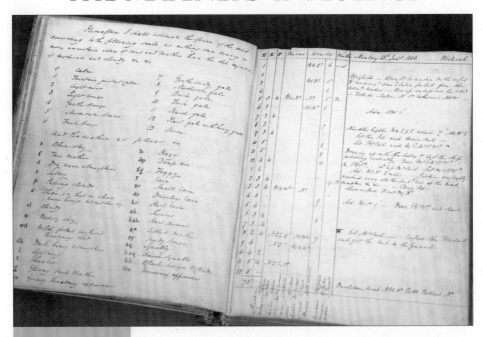

A meteorological archive showing a 19th-century daily meteorological record from Woolwich, UK. On the left-hand page is a key of the abbreviations. The Meteorological Office in Exeter, Devon, holds reports for the UK every day from January 1, 1869 to the present.

The massive expansion in colonization and trade which occurred during the 18th and 19th centuries is, arguably, responsible for the development of and the practical use of early weather recording instruments and the increase in understanding of the weather. In 1806, the British Admiral Francis Beaufort developed the Beaufort scale for measuring wind speed. Although not everyone at the time appreciated its use, it was adopted by the Royal Navy in 1838 and time has shown us how valuable it still is today. A little later than Beaufort, Royal Naval Captain (later Vice Admiral) Robert FitzRoy was responsible for developing a type of barometer that could be mass-produced and which was distributed to every port around the British Isles. During the 19th Century, the wealthy and educated were able to take advantage of the newly developing weather recording instruments to make their own conservations. Thomas Jefferson, the third president of the USA took weather readings from 1776 to 1816. If legend is to be believed, he acquired his first thermometer while writing the Declaration of Independence.

ROBERT FITZROY

Fitzroy had observed that weather systems tended to move from west to east and that low pressure could be tracked by use of an Atlantic-wide system of weather stations. The invention of the telegraph system during this time made the dissemination of the information much easier. Once appointed as Head of Meteorology, FitzRoy was able to provide the first national weather forecasts at the same time as Captain Matthew Maury was creating a similar system in the US as others were in France. FitzRoy's forecasts were published in *The Times* in London from 1860 and Queen Victoria requested a personal forecast prior to a visit to her holiday home on the Isle of Wight. Despite some setbacks FitzRoy's system was eventually approved and formed the basis of modern weather forecasting. His barometer is still in production today.

Portrait of Robert FitzRoy, RN (1805–1865), British hydrographer and meteorologist. FitzRoy was educated at the Royal Naval College at Portsmouth. He commanded HMS Beagle during both of its survey voyages to South America (1828 and 1836). During the second of these, FitzRoy took along Charles Darwin as the ship's naturalist.

THE 20TH CENTURY

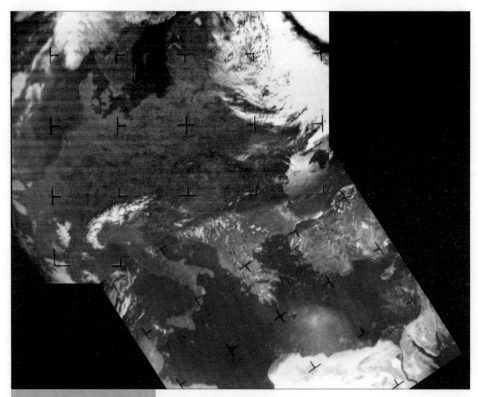

Early weather satellite images of Europe from the TIROS (Television and Infrared Observation Satellite) program (1960–1966), which used television cameras to monitor cloud patterns and the Nimbus satellites (1964–1978). These satellites were the first in a long succession of various weather satellites. Modern equipment is able to gather a much wider range of data than these early weather satellites.

The early 20th century marked the start of a transformation in the methods available to forecasters. One of the earliest pioneers in using mathematical techniques for forecasting was Lewis Fry Richardson. His interest in meteorology led him to suggest a scheme for weather forecasting using differential equations. This is the method used today but via powerful and fast computers not available to Fry at the time. When he wrote *Weather Prediction by Numerical Process* in 1922, he envisaged speeding up the calculation processes by using messengers on motorbikes to transfer information from one stage of the calculation process to another. He was also interested in atmospheric turbulence and the Richardson number, a dimensionless parameter in the theory of turbulence, is named after him.

EARLY TECHNOLOGY

The early years of the century also saw the beginnings of electronic computers, the modern versions of which we rely upon today for our forecasts. In the 1930s, aircraft were used to take upper atmosphere observations, a significant meteorological breakthrough. Because upper atmosphere pressure, wind, and temperature have a strong impact on ground level weather patterns, this was a major advance in forecasting. Another means of measuring upper atmosphere conditions is radiosonde or weather balloons, first developed during the same period but expanded rapidly during the 1940s. Radar began as a by-product of World War Two technology to track enemy aircraft during the Battle of Britain in 1940. This is now used to track oncoming rain showers and is most widely used in the USA to monitor tornadoes and hurricanes.

Scientists working on Tiros, the first weather satellite. Tiros (Television Infrared Observation Satellite) was launched on April 1, 1960. Its images of clouds led to a greater understanding of weather systems.

MODERN WEATHER
FORECASTING

WEATHER FORECASTING

Meteorologist launching a weather balloon. The balloon, which is filled with helium, carries aloft an ozonesonde, an instrument that detects ozone in the atmosphere and sends its measurements back to a base station using a radio transmitter. As the balloon gains altitude, and the local pressure drops, the balloon expands. and eventually bursts. The ozonesonde returns to Earth and provides measurements of the depletion of the ozone layer.

Modern weather forecasting uses a mixture of tried and tested weather recording instruments to provide reliable data which is then supplemented with data from satellites and radar. This data may come from automated stations or from a very large number of local manual weather stations which feed data into a national picture. Once the information is received at the various meteorological offices around the world it is processed largely by computer and fed into one of a number of computer models that have been developed as an aid to forecasting. Increasingly, forecasters are relying on ever more complex models for their predictions. The data they use may come from numerous places around the world; the various meteorological offices share information in almost real time and this reflects the unique and high degree of cooperation that exists in this field of science, originating from the days of Robert FitzRoy and his American and French colleagues in the mid-19th century.

WEATHER STATIONS

All weather stations, automated or manual, contain standard recording equipment. Inside the Stevenson's Screen, a white, louvered box on legs, are various thermometers, a barometer for recording air pressure and a hygrometer to measure humidity. In addition to these, there will be a rain and/or snow gauge, an anemometer to measure wind speed, a vane to measure wind direction and a sunshine recorder. Each will be read in a strict routine and the data sent electronically to a central meteorological office. From there each set of data is used to predict the weather and may be used as part of the data required for computer models to make longer-term predictions. In addition to these readings, weather data comes from a variety of other sources. Helium-filled weather balloons provide upper atmosphere data. Their results are transmitted to ground stations by radio hence their alternative name— radiosonde balloons. Specially equipped aircraft also collect data on temperature and humidity and can be used to study the physics of clouds. Maritime weather is usually charted by ships carrying recording instruments or by buoys, which are either moored or allowed to drift with the ocean currents.

Readings are taken every three hours from this row of Stevenson's Screens at the Arctic Reseach Station in Finnish Lapland.

THERMOMETERS

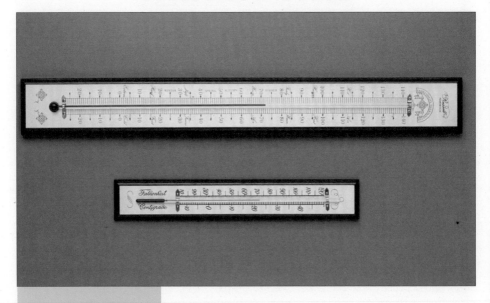

Two thermometers for measuring air temperatures. They each comprise a hollow, evacuated glass column with a bulb at the bottom which contains mercury that is dyed blue or red. The mercury expands as the air temperature increases. This means that the level of the mercury rises up the tube and can be read off using a scale.

There are several different types of thermometers in weather stations that are used by forecasters. The standard thermometer contains either mercury or alcohol: both liquids react with temperature and expand or contract at a regular, recordable rate allowing accurate measurement of temperature to be taken. A maximum–minimum (max–min) thermometer contains two separate thermometers side by side. Each one measures the current air temperature as well as the maximum—or minimum—recorded over a particular period. The small metal markers contained inside each thermometer are pushed by the liquid and remain at the maximum or minimum temperatures reached over a chosen period of time, usually one day. The markers can be reset once the temperature has been read, by either a magnet or a push-button mechanism. This type of thermometer is sometimes known as "Six's thermometer." Another type of max–min thermometer is the bimetallic dial thermometer. This has pointers on a dial which are very easy to read. It also needs to be reset after it has been read.

ANEMOMETERS

On bridges, at airports, and on many public buildings it is possible to see an instrument with rapidly revolving small cups attached. This is the most common type of anemometer, an instrument used to measure wind speed. The word anemometer derives from the Greek word "anemos" which means wind. The first anemometer was invented in the 15th century by an Italian, Leone Battista Alberti. By far the simplest device is the cup anemometer. It was invented in 1841 at an Irish Observatory by Dr John Robinson. Three or four small hemispherical cups are attached at each end of two horizontal arms which are in turn mounted on a vertical shaft. An alternative device is the hot-wire anemometer, an extremely delicate but highly accurate instrument. It uses a very fine wire, commonly of tungsten, heated to a temperature above the ambient temperature. Wind flow past the wire has a cooling effect on the wire. Using this it is possible to calculate the speed of the wind.

An anemometer—an instrument used to measure wind speed—located on top of a tower at the Jodrell Bank Radio Observatory near Manchester, England. When the wind exceeds a certain speed, the telescope is pointed straight up (as seen here) and secured.

THE STEVENSON SCREEN

A Stevenson Screen containing thermometers and other meteorological measuring and recording devices. The screen is designed to protect the thermometers from the effects of direct radiation and rainfall whilst allowing the free movement of air through the screen. The screens also ensure that conditions at different weather stations are as nearly standardized as possible, allowing a true comparison to be made between temperatures measured at different locations.

The Stevenson's Screen was designed and invented by the father of the author of *Treasure Island*, Robert Louis Stevenson. The white-painted, louver-sided box sits on legs 4 feet above the ground to avoid interference from the ground. The louvered sides allow a stable airflow through it and over the instruments it contains. It is painted white to reflect incoming radiation from the sun and has a door which opens to the north in the Northern Hemisphere and the opposite in the Southern Hemisphere, in both cases to avoid direct sunlight affecting the readings taken by the instruments. Inside are a number of crucial instruments for recording and then forecasting the weather. Dry bulb, wet bulb, and maximum–minimum thermometers are enclosed and are read in that order. The box also contains a barometer which is used to measure air pressure, a critically important part of weather forecasting.

BAROMETERS

A barometer is used to measure air pressure and thus help indicate short-term weather trends. Gases in the Earth's atmosphere have a weight and these exert a pressure on the Earth's surface. It is this pressure that is measured by a barometer. If air pressure is rising this indicates a trend toward more settled weather. When the pressure falls the likely result will be unsettled conditions, perhaps with some rain. Air pressure is most commonly measured in millibars but it can also be measured in pascals or inches of mercury. Most of the barometers found in homes are the aneroid type. These were first produced by Lucien Vidie during the 19th century. They are comprised of a corrugated metal capsule with most of the air removed. This contains an internal spring to prevent it collapsing. As the air pressure rises or falls, the capsule sides move in or out with the movement showing up on a surface dial on the face of the barometer. Whatever method of measuring air pressure, it is usual to record the readings as a trace on a specially designed sheet of graph paper with an instrument called a barograph.

A barograph, a barometer which can measure and record the atmospheric pressure as part of weather forecasting. This is an aneroid barometer in which changes in atmospheric pressure causes a bellows-like vacuum chamber (at center) to expand or contract. This deformation causes a pointer to move around the face of the graph paper to reveal the atmospheric pressure.

MONITORING SUNSHINE AND HUMIDITY

A modern sun recorder used to measure sunshine duration. It uses photo-diodes that alter an electrical signal depending on the amount of sunlight present. Electrical heaters ensure dew, frost and ice do not interfere with the readings.

A simple glass sphere is used to measure the duration and intensity of sunshine. This is a device known as the Campbell-Stokes sunshine recorder. The sphere focuses and magnifies light from the sun onto a specially treated fire-retardant card and a trace is burnt onto it if the sun is bright enough. The more sunshine there is, the longer the total length of the line.

A hygrometer measures the moisture content or humidity of the air. The first hygrometer was designed by a Swiss scientist, Horace Benedict de Saussure. The most common type of hygrometer is the dry and wet bulb thermometer. The dry bulb thermometer is mercury filled, recording changes in temperature in degrees and tenths of a degree centigrade. This is the temperature shown on television and radio forecasts. The wet bulb thermometer is an ordinary one with a muslin wick covering the bulb. This is fed by water from a special reservoir attached. The comparison between the dry and wet bulb temperatures allows the dew point, and so the relative humidity, to be calculated.

MONITORING RAINFALL

A rain gauge is used by meteorologists to collect and measure the amount of precipitation that falls over a set period of time. A separate snow gauge measures snowfall. Rain is measured in millimeters or inches, and very occasionally, in centimeters. There are numerous different versions, the most common type being the graduated cylinder rain gauge. It is this type that is usually found in amateur as well as many professional weather stations.

Meteorologists are not only interested in the amount of rain that falls, samples of rainfall are collected for analysis. A rainfall pollution monitor collects both dry and wet deposition. The dry collector has chemically-impregnated filters to collect nitric acid, sulfur dioxide and particulate pollutants. The wet collector collects rain, and other precipitation, for analysis of pollutants.

A scientist collects the water from a rainfall sampler to be sent for analysis. Measurement of the relative amounts of the oxygen-18 and hydrogen-2 (deuterium) atomic isotopes in rainwater helps to determine the global circulation of water.

RADAR

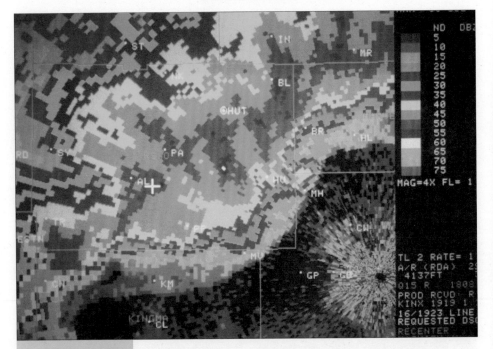

Radar image of a storm. Computer screen showing the output from a Doppler radar, a system used by meteorologists to monitor storms. The different colors represent different intensities of rainfall. A scale is shown on the right. Values of up to 30 DBZ indicate light rainfall and between 30 and 60 DBZ indicate heavy rainfall, whereas anything above 60 DBZ is likely to be hail.

In making short-term forecasts, radar has become an indispensable part of the weather forecaster's armory. Modern radar systems are able to produce, every ten or fifteen minutes, highly detailed three-dimensional pictures of weather systems such as thunderstorms or fronts and even hurricanes. Radar is the only instrument that can warn forecasters of the imminent formation of thunderstorms or tornadoes. In the US, radar is used to track the eye of hurricanes so that coastal communities have the most accurate information, such as when to evacuate prior to a land strike.

It is now possible to look at live radar images on the internet and via television forecasts.

Radar was first developed during the Second World War to help detect incoming enemy aircraft at the time of the Battle of Britain in 1940. Radar stands for "radio detection and ranging" Once it was realized that it could also detect rain it became an indispensable tool for forecasters.

HOW RADAR WORKS

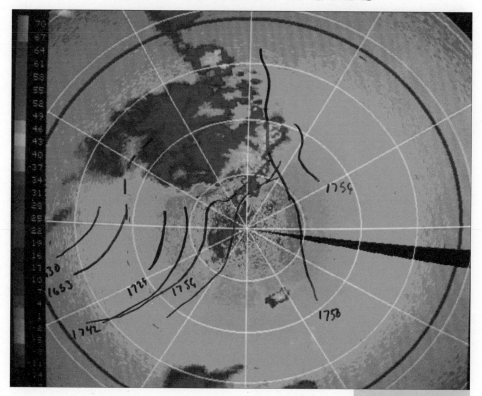

Radar works by transmitting pulses of radio waves from an antenna. When it meets a "target" such as a rain shower some of the beam is reflected back. A Doppler radar measures the change in frequency of the returned echoes which allows for wind speeds to be calculated. Radar devices such as these have a very narrow beam which, when scanning the atmosphere at different angles, can produce a three-dimensional picture of the weather.

The USA has the most comprehensive system of weather radar in the world which is used to monitor the 10,000 violent storms, 5000 floods and as many as 1000 tornadoes it experiences every year. They use aircraft such as the Electra L188L to get as close as possible to the center of developing storms and so provide a detailed three-dimensional image of the wind and rainfall inside it.

Radar image of a storm cloud (red and yellow). This radar is used to monitor an armored aircraft as it flies through a thunderstorm to collect research data.

SATELLITES

False-color weather satellite photograph of Hurricane Allen over the Gulf of Mexico.

Since the launch of the first satellite in the 1950s there has been the exciting possibility of using them to monitor and help predict the weather. The first weather satellite was the 1960 TIROS 1, followed in 1966 by the first equatorial orbiting satellite, essential for monitoring severe weather such as hurricanes. Today satellites such as the METEOSAT geostationary or global orbiting satellites are an essential part of the modern forecaster's tools. They provide a continuous feed of data from all parts of the globe, including those that in the past had been too remote or inhospitable such as deserts and oceans.

All satellites are useful in monitoring and tracking particular aspects of the weather such as the intense and dangerous hurricanes or tropical cyclones to the more routine high and low pressure systems. They can also be used to measure wind speeds and to analyze cloud patterns.

Without a doubt, the development of modern satellites has become an increasingly important tool for both forecasting the day-to-day weather and in helping to make climate predictions. The newest generation of satellites being launched during the early years of the 21st century may prove invaluable if predicted changes in global climate prove true.

TYPES OF SATELLITE

There are two main types of satellites in common usage today. The geostationary satellites are positioned at a height of 22,214 miles above the Equator and remain at the same spot above the Earth's surface all the time METEOSAT is the geostationary satellite operated by European countries and is positioned at the intersection of 0 degrees latitude and 0 degrees longitude, in other words, where the Greenwich Meridian intersects the Equator. From this vantage point it monitors Africa, the Middle East, Europe, much of the Atlantic, and the western Indian Ocean.

The second satellite is the Polar Orbiting type which orbits the Earth via the Poles. The NOAA satellites operated by the USA, orbit at a height of 500 miles, taking about 1 hour and 42 minutes to complete each orbit. The satellite views a different part of the Earth during each orbit as, whilst on its journey, the Earth has rotated through 22 degrees. During 2006 Metop, a European satellite will replace one of the NOAAs. With such a low orbit the satellite can record far more detail than that of the geostationary types.

Technicians working on the METEOSAT 6 weather satellite at the Aerospatiale test facility in Toulouse, France. A full-disk image of the Earth is returned every 30 minutes from its geostationary orbit.

MAPPING WEATHER

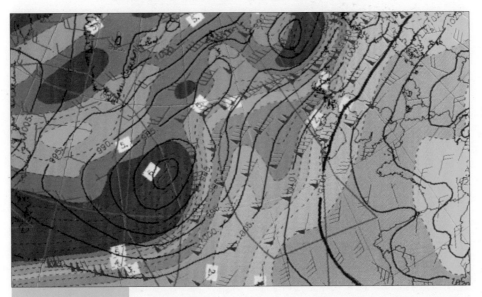

Computer simulation of a weather map which forms part of the FASTEX (Fronts and Atlantic Storm Tracks Experiment) weather study. The solid lines show isobars which link areas of equal pressure; the closer the isobars appear on the map, the higher the winds will be in these areas. The FASTEX study uses data from aircraft, ships and satellites to discover what factors turn a normal low-pressure weather system (cyclone) into a storm.

A synoptic chart shows the weather for a particular area at a specific time. It is the result of the collection of a mass of data from numerous weather stations. These are refined, usually by computer, and plotted using a range of internationally accepted weather symbols. There are several different types of synoptic charts. The most sophisticated is one which has a huge amount of detail covering, for example, the amount of cloud of various types at different altitudes, dew point temperatures and pressure trends. These are highly specialized and would normally be used only at a national or regional weather forecasting centers Before the use of computers, drawing such a map was considered something of an art which some aerographers (weather men) in the US Navy continue to do.

Today, however, the daily weather map is the one people are most likely to come across in the media. This aims to give a clear, if highly simplified and general, impression of the weather. Despite the array of information at their disposal forecasters can still claim only as much as 70 percent accuracy in their forecasts shown on these maps. Weather data is a sample taken at different locations rather than a total picture.

METEOROLOGICAL OFFICES

All around the world people depend upon an accurate weather forecast, from the ordinary citizen to more specialist users such as farmers, shipping, or aviation companies. These forecasts depend upon accurate and extensive data collection which is both organized and processed by national meteorological offices around the world. Virtually every country has a national meteorological service, from the Australian Bureau of Meteorology to Pakistan's Meteorological Department. Some countries have, in addition to a national service, forecasting institutions such as in the USA where there is the National Weather Service in Maryland as well as organizations such as the Weather Information from the Department of Meteorology of the University of Hawaii. In the United Kingdom, the Meteorological Office (Met Office), now based in Exeter, has existed since the 19th century, originally developing as a branch of the Board of Trade's forecasting service which began under the guidance of Vice Admiral FitzRoy in the 1860s. It, along with all the others, now relies very heavily on the enormous range of data collected from around the country, from at sea, and via other meteorological offices.

Weather forecasters monitor atmospheric conditions around the world to predict future weather conditions.

INTERNATIONAL COOPERATION

View of the main building (background) and instrument domes of the Mauna Loa atmospheric research station in Hawaii, USA. The open dome houses solar radiation instruments which measure the effects of atmospheric dust on sunlight. The observatory monitors all atmospheric constituents that may contribute to climatic change, such as greenhouse gases and aerosols, and those which cause depletion of the ozone layer.

Weather forecasts often depend on data from other countries and international cooperation is increasingly important. It is not a new phenomenon: in the mid-19th century Vice Admiral FitzRoy of the British Royal Navy began his first rudimentary forecasts in the 1860s. He exchanged data and methodology with the fledgling American Meteorological service led by Captain Matthew Maury as well as the newly developing Meteorological services in France and Germany. International cooperation is now an essential part of predicting not only the weather but future climate. World Weather Watch is one such organization. The World Meteorological Organisation, with 187 members, is another and is a branch of the United Nations. As the weather knows no boundaries, and as concern about global climate change grows, organizations such as these will surely play an increasingly important role in the future.

WEATHER BROADCASTING

Weather forecasts that appear on television, the radio, in newspapers and on the internet have become so much a part of our daily lives. The modern weather forecast began during the mid-19th century when the British Meteorological Office (Met Office), a branch of the Board of Trade, was established in 1854. The Met Office started issuing gale warnings to shipping in 1861. Some rudimentary forecasts were published in the London *Times*. Formal weather forecasts were published widely in the press from 1879.

In November 1922 the BBC broadcast its first radio weather forecast with regular broadcasts beginning in March of the following year. On November 11, 1936 the BBC transmitted the world's first ever televised weather forecast.

Since then weather forecast broadcasting has been transformed. World-wide television and radio services produce regular forecasts of varying lengths and degrees of detail.

Historical photograph of Ben Nevis Observatory, the first high-altitude meteorological station in Britain, which opened in 1883. Ben Nevis is the highest mountain in Britain, standing 4410 feet tall. The observatory was set up to measure the weather at altitude, but it was closed in 1904 as a result of a lack of funds.

HARNESSING
THE WEATHER

RENEWABLES

Rooftop solar heat collectors (large black panels) in Stettlen, Switzerland that are using the heat in sunlight to heat water supplies for each house. This saves energy and reduces heating costs. It also avoids the use of power-generation methods that produce pollution, such as burning fossil fuels.

Harnessing the weather to create energy is hardly new. Humans have been making use of the sun, water, and wind for thousands of years to create heat for transport, farming, and industry. The Greek island of Karpathos has used windmills for hundreds of years and still does today; the sight of windmills in many parts of the Netherlands is an iconic image of the country, even if their use is now not very widespread.

As supplies of endangered fossil fuels become more precarious and the concern about the pollution they generate has grown, we are increasingly returning to the idea of using weather-related "renewables." The technology of solar, wind, and hydro-electricity production has advanced and what were once seen as marginal energy sources are now becoming increasingly important. Of course, all these sources of energy are weather dependent.

CLOUD SEEDING

In 1946 in Massachusetts, USA, an experiment took place to discover whether it was possible to increase the amount of precipitation that falls from clouds. An aeroplane "seeded" a cloud with crushed dry ice (frozen carbon dioxide) and snow fell from it. A little later it was discovered that silver iodide had the same potential effect and is now used as an alternative "seed."

In areas of the world where rainfall totals are low and where populations are growing (meaning agricultural output has to increase), any means by which more can be produced is welcomed. The conventional way of doing this is via irrigation schemes using large-scale dams and reservoirs but in some places the more unusual step of "cloud seeding" weather modification, has been used.

The largest system is in China where they fire rockets into the atmosphere to increase the amount of rain that falls over arid areas of the country, as well as Beijing, the capital. In the US, cloud seeding is used to increase the amount of rain over drought-prone areas, to decrease the size of hailstones that form in thunderstorms and to reduce fog around airports. It is also used occasionally to increase the amount of snow over ski resorts.

The Russian Myasishchev M-17 was designed primarily for map-making photography and for hail control. In the latter role, the aircraft "seeds" thunder-clouds with small crystals. This causes the cloud to release its rain or hail before it reaches crop areas where the hail could cause major damage.

SOLAR POWER

Humans have used solar power in a very basic form for drying clothes and crops for thousands of years. It is only recently, however, that modern technology has allowed for solar power to be generated almost anywhere, even in high latitudes. Large-scale power stations remain in lower latitudes, however, where the sun's rays are more intense and cloud cover is lower. This means that the amount of insolation or sunlight received is high enough to generate either heat, for hot water, or to generate electricity.

There are three ways in which solar energy is generated. The first of these is by use of solar cells—photovoltaic cells—which can convert light into heat to generate electricity. These are used in very sunny areas of the world such as California and southern France. The technology remains relatively expensive and so it not yet used widely in a domestic environment.

Solar water heating via solar panels are perhaps the most commonly used. These use solar energy to heat water for washing, or even for central heating if the sunshine is reliable enough. But it is more likely they will heat the water sufficiently to require little extra conventional heating to get to an appropriate temperature.

A third way is via solar furnaces, a huge array of mirrors which concentrate the Sun's energy into a small space and so produce very high temperatures. The one in Odellio, France has been able to generate temperatures as high as 59,500°F.

The advantages are obvious but then so are the disadvantages—at night there is no sun and so no energy. When it is cloudy or in higher latitude areas the energy generated is low and insufficient for anything other than small-scale, low-power uses. This does not mean, however, that in the future most homes will not be able to make use of this technology to supplement or even replace the more conventional energy sources.

Dish-shaped solar power reflectors at a solar power station at White Cliffs, Australia. Each dish focuses radiation from the sun onto a thermoelectric generator positioned in the focal point. A computer steers the dishes to ensure they face the sun throughout the day.

WIND POWER

The sight of windmills in the countryside of Britain, the Netherlands, Spain or Greece is viewed today as somewhat quaint, traditional and rustic but they show how valuable a source of energy the wind has been in the past and hint at how important it could be in the future.

Early windmills used a system of sails to turn a rotor attached to a series of cogs and wheels. These were in turn attached to millstones which rotated to grind wheat and corn into flour. Sometimes these were used to power the bellows of iron forges. This traditional system is still used in many communities today.

Modern wind farms are a very different prospect. Turbines vary in size from 80 to 200 feet high with rotor blades up to 210 feet in diameter so their visual impact is significant. Essentially, a wind turbine is an electrical generator mounted at the top of a tower. The wind causes the propeller blades to turn which rotate a central shaft connected to a generator. This makes them unpopular in some areas: environmentalists complain about the effect on migrating birds and those living near wind farms complain of the noise from the rotating blades. They are, of course, wind-dependent. If there is no wind there is no electricity. Similarly, if the wind is too strong the generators may be switched off. A large number of turbines is needed to generate enough wind to make the farm viable and ways of storing surplus energy is needed.

In 2005 world wide energy production from wind power was only 1 percent, although, in Denmark it is 23 percent and 8 percent in Spain. Global wind power generation is on the increase: between 1999 and 2005 it more than quadrupled. Due to the controversial nature of their sites on land, numerous off-shore farms have been constructed or are in the planning stage. Small-scale domestic generators are also becoming increasingly economic, efficient, and more widely-used.

View of wind turbines on a harbour wall silhouetted against the glow of a sunrise. Each turbine has three blades which rotate around a horizontal axis, turning a shaft which drives an electric generator. The blades have to be turned to face directly into the wind to work efficiently. Wind turbines are an environmentally-friendly source of energy, as they release no toxic waste products and do not rely on a limited resource for fuel.

HYDRO-ELECTRICITY

At present this is the most commonly used method of generating power from water. Of course, water power has been used for many centuries to generate energy for such things as grinding corn in mills and to power machinery. The first house to be powered by hydro-electricity was Cragside House in Northumbria, UK in 1878. By 1882 the Fox River in the USA generated enough energy to power a house and two papermills. Today, however, it is done on a very large scale where a dam is constructed which holds back a massive volume of water in a reservoir. Hydro-electricity is pollution-free and safe, once in place. In the process of construction, however, there can be immense disruption to people's lives and to the environment— villages, even towns can be permanently flooded and wildlife habitats destroyed.

The Three Gorges Dam in China is perhaps the most famous and, arguably, the most controversial hydro-electric power scheme in the world at present. Located on the Yangtse River near Yichang, construction began in 1993 and was largely completed during 2003. It is predicted to produce about 18 gigawatts to help meet the Chinese population's rapidly growing energy needs when it comes fully on line in 2009. At the outset it was hoped the scheme would provide China with 10 percent of its needs but such has been the extraordinary growth of the country's economy it is now believed it will be only 3 percent. The scheme will also improve navigation and reduce the flood risk downstream in the Yangtse valley, but it has created numerous problems for the local population. Almost 2 million people have been displaced due to the flooding of the area to create the vast lake required to store the fuel—water. Some 20,000 acres of the best farmland has gone for ever and the habitat of rare species such as the Chinese River Dolphin has also disappeared for good, putting this and other species at risk of extinction.

A hydro-electric watermill. It has incorporated a turbine for electricity generation since 1888. The technology behind the water mill is somewhat older than the windmill. Both the Greeks and Romans are known to have used this technology.

PAST
CLIMATES

CLIMATE TRENDS

Fossil remains of Archaeopteryx. It was found in the fine-grained limestones of the late Jurassic period (195–135 million years ago) at Solenhofen, Bavaria. Archaeopteryx, seen as the link between reptile and bird, had many of the features of a small dinosaur with the addition of feathers and combined reptilian and bird-like claws on its wings. It was approximately the size of a crow.

Around 4.6 billion years ago our Earth was formed. At some point up to about 2.7 billion years ago glaciers and ice sheets began to develop. Since then the Earth has undergone numerous minor and major climate shifts. The last 65 million years is known as the Cenozoic Era; during most of this time the Earth has undergone a period of cooling, albeit rather irregular in pattern. The part of the Cenozoic Era that we are currently in is known as the Quaternary geological period which began about 1.6 million years ago. The first part of this, the Pleistocene period, saw seven major glaciations during which as much as 30 percent of the Earth was covered by ice at any one time. The current part is the Holocene Epoch which is a time of warm temperatures that began about 10,000 years ago. It is possible that this is an interglacial period, one that exists between glacial periods. The mass of evidence that suggests the Earth's atmosphere is warming due to human action may well be true but we ought to be aware that we have seen fluctuations like this in the past. It is highly possible that, despite the apparent evidence, we still do not yet know what lies ahead for our climate.

THE PALAEOZOIC ERA

Around 370 million years ago the first sedimentary rocks such as limestone, sandstone, and chalk were laid down under the sea or at the bottom of lakes. At this time the Earth's temperatures were about 18°F higher than today. The first life forms, algae, were formed about 3.5 billion years ago. From that time onward until the Mesozoic Era—the time of the dinosaurs—about 250 to about 65 million years ago, the Earth warmed then cooled repeatedly. This led to periods of intense glaciation which were followed by periods of warmer conditions. We have evidence of this from the sedimentary rocks laid down during these periods. Plant fossils preserved in the rocks indicate that the climate during the pre-dinosaur period was much warmer and more humid than today. Much of the fossil evidence remaining is of ferns; these plants need warm and humid conditions to survive and their remains, laid down first in the Devonian and also in the Carboniferous period (from 345–280 million years ago) provide evidence of that. Many of the coal deposits laid down in the Carboniferous period and mined during the 19th and 20th centuries contain fossilized seed ferns.

View of a cliff of sedimentary rock in Zion National Park, Utah, USA, showing very distinct strata. The upper layers of the rocks were deposited about 10 million years ago, whilst the lowest layers are over 250 million years old. The rocks are different colors due to their composition: most of the red and yellow rocks are sandstones with differing amounts of mineral inclusions. The prominent gray layer is from the Chinle formation, a graywacke deposit from the late Triassic period of about 210 million years ago, in which dinosaur footprints have been found.

THE MESOZOIC ERA

Ancient Earth. Computer artwork of the Earth at the time of the death of the dinosaurs, some 65 million years ago. The continents of North America (top center), South America (lower center) and Africa (center right) are seen. The position and shape of the continents has changed over time due to continental drift, erosion and climate change.

The film *Jurassic Park* and its sequels reflect our continuing interest in the dinosaur period, the Mesozoic Era. The Triassic and Jurassic geological periods saw the evolution of a wide range of dinosaur species made possible by the presence of warm seas. Such sea conditions are usually associated with higher rainfall totals over the land which can encourage lush vegetation growth and in turn encourage the development of huge herbivore dinosaur species. Toward the end of the Triassic period the Earth was subjected to massive upheaval caused by continental drift—the gradual "drifting" of the Earth's continents across the globe. It would have had major effects on global ocean currents and on continental temperatures. It is speculated that this may have had an effect on growing conditions and the availability of food for the dinosaurs and so was perhaps responsible for their extinction.

ICE AGES

Periods of glaciation—ice ages—have been regular occurrences in the Earth's history. The evidence suggests that these occur approximately every 200 to 250 million years on average and that they have lasted for millions of years. A period of glaciation consists of major climate differences between the Poles and the equatorial regions. During an ice age the ice at the Poles extends into lower latitudes creating extensive ice sheets across the land and the sea as well as the development of huge valley glaciers. In this, the Quaternary phase of the Cenozoic Era, the Earth has experienced three significant periods of cooling at about 36, 15, and 3 million years ago. There is a huge array of geological evidence to show that ice once covered huge areas of the Earth that are now ice free. Deep, steep-sided U-shaped valleys, often with mounds of debris called moraine on their floors and at their sides were left behind when the ice melted; these can still be seen today in places such as northern Europe and parts of North and South America. It is possible to identify glacial processes currently operating in place that still have ice today. The resulting landforms can then be seen in other parts of the world and can provide some of the evidence for climate change.

A glacier is a huge mass of ice formed of compacted snow, moving slowly over a land mass. As a glacier retreats, it leaves behind piles of such rocks, called glacial moraine. A glacier retreats when it melts faster than snow accumulates.

MILANKOVITCH CYCLES

Serbian astrophysicist, Milutin Milankovitch dedicated his career to developing a mathematical theory of climate based on the seasonal and latitudinal variations in solar radiation received by the Earth. The resulting Milankovitch Theory states that there are cyclical variations between the Earth and the Sun which affect the amount of solar radiation reaching the Earth. The Earth's orbit, already slightly elliptical, is believed to change shape at regular intervals. At some period of time the orbit around the Sun is more elliptical and so it receives less solar radiation. The angle at which the Earth's axis lies with the plane of orbit is currently 23.44°. Milankovitch believed that this angle changes periodically and that it could be between 21.5° and 24.5°. This would also affect the amount of solar radiation received by the Earth and so lead to warming or cooling cycles.

Milankovitch also identified 100,000 year ice age cycles of the Quaternary Glaciation period over the last few million years. He believed that there would be one full period of precession every 26,000 years; in other words there would be a change in the direction of the Earth's axis of rotation during that time. This behaves in a similar way to that of a spinning top as it winds down; it traces a circle on the celestial sphere over a period of time.

Global ocean circulation. Satellite image of the Earth from space with a map of ocean circulation. Ocean currents flow around the world due to differences in temperature and salinity. A current of warm water (red) from the Pacific Ocean travels westward on the ocean surface. As it flows, it evaporates and becomes saltier. The Gulf Stream carries the warm, salty water up along the East Coast of the United States, then towards Europe. At colder northern latitudes, the water becomes so dense that it sinks to the sea floor and travels south (blue). Disruption of the Gulf Stream from global warming could result in ice-age conditions in Europe.

ICE CORES

Scientists collecting a 33 feet ice core, drilled from the Antarctic near the Rothera Research Station. Chemical analysis of ice cores can reveal changes in climate over several hundreds of years. Air trapped in the firn (the upper layer of frozen snow) is untainted by the atmospheric air, and thus provides direct evidence of what the composition of the atmosphere was at the time when the firn froze.

It is not easy to find out about the climate of the distant past, but there are several ways in which it can be done. One such way of finding out is by taking samples of ice from the Arctic and Antarctic. These are called ice cores, which are drilled from the surface of the ice deep into the ice at depths of up to 2 miles. At this depth the ice can be up to 100,000 years old consisting of compressed snow which fell at that time. The snow never melts and so the differences between summer and winter accumulation is very evident, which explains why the ice cores are so useful in showing seasonal and long-term climate changes. Anything else that was in the atmosphere at the time will be deposited along with the snow, such as ash that fell from Krakatoa in 1883 or even earlier deposits from lead smelters in Roman times. Pollen that fell with the snow can show what plant species were common at different times in the past, reflecting variations in climate. In addition to this, and a very important recent source of information, is the natural variations in dissolved acids and salts along with gases and liquids trapped in the minute air bubbles in the ice. Studying the variations in "greenhouse" gases such as carbon dioxide is proving a very useful tool in tracking past climates and so in the potential for predicting future changes.

SEDIMENTARY EVIDENCE

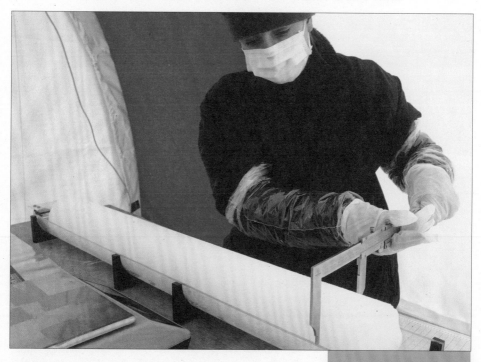

Sediments from sea or lake beds can be extracted by the same process used with ice cores. In a similar way the sediments act as a record of the amount and type of material deposited. In a very dry period the layers of sediment are likely to be very thin whereas in a much wetter period the opposite is likely to be the case. The size of the sediment particles can also provide a clue since larger sediments can only be moved if there is sufficient energy in the streams entering the lake or sea to pick them up. In March 2003, an article in *Science* magazine suggested that lake sediments from Mexico and Venezuela provide the evidence that a series of droughts occurred between 810 and 910 AD. These dates correlate well with the known abandonment of Mayan cities and it has been suggested that the civilisation collapsed due to the droughts.

Researcher measuring an ice core to help determine its density, which in turn helps to date the ice. The ice formed over 1000 years ago from the compaction of snow. Analysis of the ice can provide information about the climatic conditions in which it formed. Cores can reveal changes in climate and atmospheric composition over thousands of years. Knowing how the climate changed in the past allows more accurate predictions of future changes. This core was taken during the EPICA (European Project for Ice Coring in Antarctica) from the ice at Dronning Maud Land, Antarctica.

DENDROCHRONOLOGY

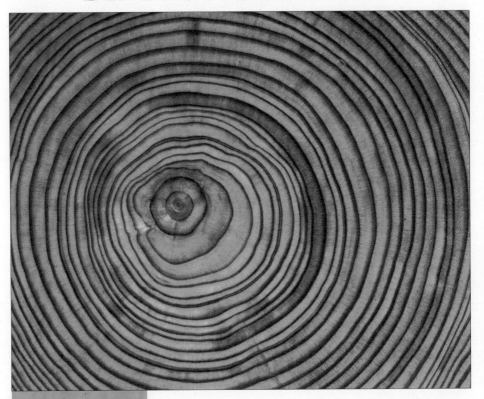

Each year the outer, living part of a tree trunk lays down a new layer of water-conducting xylem cells. The older cells dry out and die, forming the hard mass of wood in the core of the trunk. Each ring corresponds to a single year, so the tree's age can be determined by counting the rings. Climatic fluctuations from year to year result in distinctive patterns of wide and narrow rings, which are repeated in different trees.

The study of dendrochronology, or tree rings is a well used source of evidence for past climates. Each year's growth is recorded in a clearly discernible ring which is a record of the climate and growth conditions of that time. It can reflect the precipitation, sun, wind, soil, temperature and snow fall experienced in the area where the tree grew. Variations in the size of the tree rings show when the tree has been affected by drought or lack of sunlight caused by major events such as volcanic eruptions for example. Such records go back to the end of the last ice age, some 10,000 years ago. The oldest living trees are the bristlecones of California, known to live for up to 5000 years and so provide a major source of information.

THE LITTLE ICE AGE

Understanding the climate of the more recent past is significantly easier. We have a massive body of organized, historical weather records to act as evidence for changing weather and climate over the past few centuries. Records of wide-spread famine, advancing Alpine glaciers and freezing of the River Thames in London—reveal a temporary cooling of the Earth's atmosphere during the 17th and 18th century. This "little ice age" caused the Baltic Sea and major rivers like the Thames to regularly freeze over. "Frost fairs" were held on the Thames during this time. In 1564 the earliest record of people using the frozen river for entertainment such as archery competitions emerges but that they really took off during the 17th century. In 1685 the Thames was frozen for two months and enterprising businessmen set up stalls selling food. Riverboat men, the taxi drivers of the day, struggled to make a living and resorted to breaking holes in the ice and charging people to cross from the river bank to the solid ice of the frozen river. Even King Charles II and his family visited in this year, reflecting the popularity of the event. More frost fairs followed in the years 1715–6, 1739–40 and 1813–14, the last "proper" frost fair. The peak period of the Little Ice Age was between 1550 and 1750.

Lone tree on top of a hill called a drumlin. This is a feature formed by the action of a glacier. This drumlin is near Menzingen, Switzerland, and was formed by the Linth Glacier that advanced over this area in the last Ice Age some 10,000 years ago.

FUTURE
CLIMATES

CLIMATE CHANGE

The Earth's atmosphere is in a cycle of constant but very slow change. Much well-documented evidence exists to prove that climate has altered many times in the past. This includes glaciated valleys and mountains, sand dunes, and geological evidence such as fossils and coal deposits, the relics of ancient tropical forests. The idea of future climate change should not, therefore, come as any great surprise.

Climate change has always been thought to be gradual and slow. It is believed that the last Ice Age ended 10,000 years ago and that it took many centuries for the ice to gradually disappear. It was, until recently, thought that there had been climatic fluctuations over short periods lasting 30 to 100 years but around a relative norm similar to that which has existed for the last 4000 years.

However, in recent years doubt has been cast on these assumptions and climate change is now a matter of great concern and serious public, national, and international debate. One of the main issues is that human activity may be responsible for not only a change but also an increase in the rate of climate change. In addition, it is now recognized that climate change in the past almost certainly occurred much more swiftly than had previously been thought, in other words in as short a time as a century rather than over many centuries.

The greatest concern now is that these changes are leading to a significant increase in global temperatures. Recent research suggests that the Earth's average temperature has risen by 1°F since 1960 and by 1°F since the start of the Industrial Revolution. Concern about the effects of global warming has inevitably increased in recent years. Governments have signed treaties such as the Kyoto Protocol of 1997 and had discussions more recently at the Bonn conference of 2006 in order to minimize the amount of greenhouse gases being emitted into the atmosphere in an attempt to reduce the risk of future climate change.

Type II polar stratospheric clouds (PSC II), seen from a NASA DC-8 research aircraft over the Arctic. The bright PCS IIs are at an altitude of 50,000 feet and are composed of crystals of water ice. The clouds exhibit a "wave" structure, caused by the effect of mountains on the winds that move the clouds. PSCs are found in the circumpolar vortex winds that circle both poles. Type I PSCs (made of nitric acid crystals) have been linked with the chemical processes that are depleting the ozone layers over the Arctic and Antarctic regions.

ACID RAIN

During the 1970s and 1980s the Scandinavian countries of northern Europe reported significant damage to their coniferous forests and lakes. Forests were dying and the lakes, streams, and soil were becoming increasingly acidic. It was believed that the death of the trees was also due to the highly acidic nature of the rainfall over the area. The blame was put at the door of countries further south, particularly the UK, which had been burning fossil fuels for many decades. The prevailing south-westerly winds had blown the resulting gases across the Scandinavian countries where they fell as acid rain.

Acid rain is something of a broad term as it can refer to either wet or dry deposition. What they have in common is a greater than normal concentration of nitric and sulfuric acid. This can occur naturally, such as when volcanoes erupt, but it is the anthropogenic sort, that caused by human activity, that is usually discussed. When fossil fuels such as coal are combusted they release gases such as sulfur dioxide and nitrogen dioxide. These gases react in the atmosphere with water vapor, oxygen, and other chemicals to form various acidic compounds. The result is mild sulfuric or nitric acid released in rainfall or acid fog or mist as well as acid snow.

The dry form occurs when sulfur dioxide and nitrogen dioxide are released during combustion and are blown across national borders by the prevailing winds. It is estimated that about 50 percent of all acidity in the atmosphere occurs in the dry form. These chemicals may become incorporated into the soil as well as into streams and lakes. Some will land on trees and vegetation where it can be washed off by rain, which it in turn becomes acidic.

A conifer forest on Mount Mitchell in North Carolina, USA, with many trees damaged or killed by acid rain. Loss of leaves and stunted growth occur as the trees undergo a "die back" effect. Trees, especially conifers, are particularly vulnerable to acid rain.

THE EFFECTS OF ACID RAIN

Acid rain doesn't directly kill trees and other vegetation; rather it weakens them by damaging leaves which means they cannot easily access nutrients. Acid water dissolves some soluble nutrients and minerals in the soil and leaches them out, in other words it washes them out into lower layers of the soil where the vegetation roots cannot reach them.

Acid rain can also have a noticeable effect on buildings and other structures made of alkaline materials such as limestone. Sir Christopher Wren's St Paul's Cathedral in London was built using a form of limestone sometimes called Purbeck marble; the stone is of the very highest order with an almost marble-like appearance. However, the increasingly acidic atmosphere over London has scarred the building: it is estimated that the acid rain and dry acid compounds that fall on the Cathedral dissolve the stone to the equivalent of a bucketful each day. The lead plugs used in its construction during the 17th century now stand about an inch above the surface of the building, reflecting the rapid rate of weathering since its construction. Similar effects can be seen on churches and other public buildings, even gravestones, caused by acidification of the atmosphere.

The effects of acid rain and its variants on human health are sometimes overlooked but they can be serious. It is the polluting compounds, sulfur dioxide and nitrogen dioxides, in the atmosphere rather than the acidic water itself that are the source of the problem. These gases interact in the atmosphere to form fine sulfate and nitrate particles that can be inhaled deep into people's lungs. Numerous scientific studies have suggested a link between elevated particles and increased illness, even deaths, from heart or lung disorders such as asthma and bronchitis.

Nitrogen oxides are also known to interact with volatile organic compounds to form ozone which impacts on human health causing an increase in the risks associated with lung inflammation including asthma and emphysema.

Relief work on the facade of St Bartholomew's Church in midtown Manhattan, New York, damaged from years of pollution and acid rain.

THE GREENHOUSE EFFECT

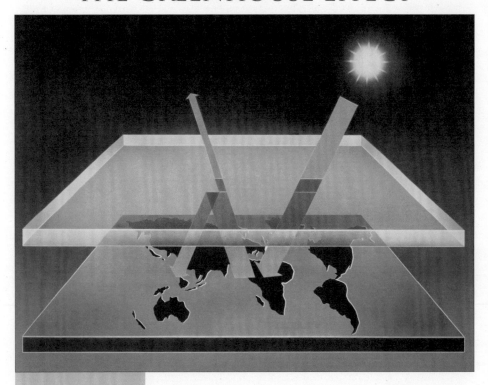

Illustration of the "greenhouse effect." The build-up of certain gases in Earth's immediate atmosphere—the troposphere—traps an increased amount of solar radiation and leads to a gradual warming of the whole planet. Here, a polluted troposphere is represented by the purple band, allowing only a small fraction of re-radiated solar energy (yellow arrows) to return to space.

The Earth is made habitable by "greenhouse" gases such as carbon dioxide, ozone and methane. These gases absorb infrared radiation and warm the planet, making it habitable for human and other life. When the balance of greenhouse gases changes as a result of human activity, the so-called enhanced greenhouse effect occurs, an idea first explored by Joseph Fourrier in 1824. The Earth receives energy from the Sun in the form of radiation, mainly in the visible spectrum. Much of this, about 70 percent, is absorbed by the land, atmosphere, and water on the Earth's surface but eventually much is re-radiated back into space. About 30 percent of the incoming energy is reflected back into space before it reaches the land. This regular cycle keeps the Earth in balance. If that balance is disturbed the Earth may either cool down or heat up. Minor fluctuation is part of the normal process but it is the threat of major imbalances that is of real concern.

GREENHOUSE GASES

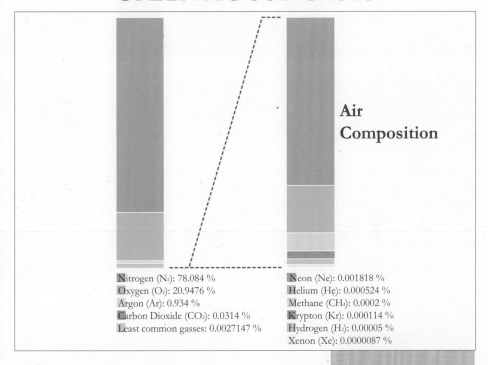

**Air
Composition**

Nitrogen (N₂): 78.084 %
Oxygen (O₂): 20.9476 %
Argon (Ar): 0.934 %
Carbon Dioxide (CO₂): 0.0314 %
Least common gasses: 0.0027147 %

Neon (Ne): 0.001818 %
Helium (He): 0.000524 %
Methane (CH₄): 0.0002 %
Krypton (Kr): 0.000114 %
Hydrogen (H₂): 0.00005 %
Xenon (Xe): 0.0000087 %

The main "greenhouse" gases are water vapor, methane, nitrous oxide, and carbon dioxide with a significant contribution made by ozone and chlorofluorocarbons.

Since the Industrial Revolution there has been a marked increase in the amount of carbon dioxide, nitrous oxide, and methane in the atmosphere. Recent data from the Mauna Loa Observatory suggest that CO_2 levels have increased from 313 ppm in 1960 to 375 ppm in 2005.

Global climate models suggest that the increase in CO_2 levels may be responsible for a warming of the Earth's atmosphere which it is believed has increased by 1°F in the last 150 years, of which 1°F is since 1960. A considerable body of evidence is being amassed to support the argument that human activity is responsible for this warming but the issue remains controversial.

Diagram showing the composition of air. The greenhouse gases in the atmosphere keep the Earth's average surface temperature at about 59°F. Without them the temperature would be closer to 0°F, far too low to support life. The atmosphere keeps the Earth warm in a way which is similar, but not identical, to the way a greenhouse keeps plants warm.

THE OZONE LAYER

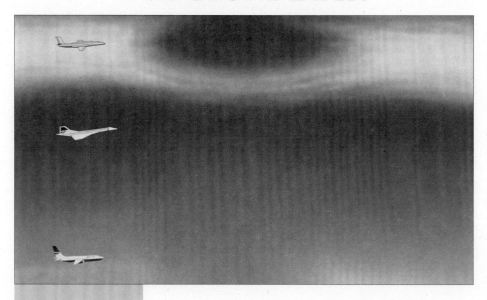

Artwork showing the severe depletion or "hole" in the ozone layer over Antarctica. The ozone layer occurs at an altitude of 9–15 miles, but is most concentrated at 11–13 miles (shown in white). The hole lets through the UV radiation (purple). Altitudes are given by a Boeing 727 (7 miles), a Concorde (9 miles), and the ER-2 research plane (11 miles) used by NASA to investigate the hole. The hole first appeared in 1980, and has grown more severe each year. It is a seasonal phenomenon that occurs in the Antarctic spring.

Ozone enables the human race to exist yet can make our lives very difficult indeed. Ozone is a gas that is made up of atoms of oxygen. It can exist anywhere in the atmosphere but is mostly concentrated in the stratosphere at around 14 miles or higher above the Earth where it provides a protective barrier against the Sun's potentially harmful ultraviolet rays. Under certain atmospheric conditions it can also be formed near ground level. Normal oxygen consists of two atoms but ozone comprises three and has the chemical formula O_3. It is sometimes pale blue in color and has a quite strong smell. It is also highly poisonous.

During the late 1970s, scientists working for the British Antarctic Survey found that the amount of high-level ozone had decreased quite significantly over the continent. The so-called ozone hole is a periodic one that opens in the Antarctic spring and closes several months later. Research carried out in the Arctic discovered a smaller but very similar pattern of ozone depletion occurring there too.

CHLOROFLUOROCARBONS

The responsible agent for depletion of the ozone layer is a group of chemicals called chlorofluorocarbons (CFCs) used commonly as refrigerants and in aerosol sprays. These chemicals are also used in air conditioning units, cleaning solvents, and packaging materials such as polystyrene. The CFCs reach the upper atmosphere where they react with sunlight to produce a gas called chlorine monoxide which is highly reactive and acts as a catalyst for the breakdown of ozone.

In 1985 the Montreal Protocol was signed by 49 countries following a United Nations convention. The idea was to phase out the use of CFCs by the end of the 20th century. In 1989 the EU proposed a total ban on the use of CFCs by the end of the 1990s. Research continues and in 1991 NASA launched a satellite to measure and monitor the variations in ozone at different altitudes, with the intention of providing a more complete picture. Although the amount of CFCs in the atmosphere has been dramatically cut since the 1990s the problem persists; the chemicals have a long life and can remain in the atmosphere for more than 80 years; so damage to the ozone layer may last for a long time to come. This means that the Earth is exposed to far more UV radiation that is either necessary or safe.

Refrigerators and freezers stacked ready for recycling at a refuse disposal site. The machines have their compressors, coolant (refrigerant) and polyurethane foam removed before they are crushed and sold for scrap. The coolants and foam contain chlorofluorocarbon (CFC) chemicals. CFCs are harmful gases that deplete the ozone layer and can trap heat in the atmosphere, which may contribute to the greenhouse effect.

LOW-LEVEL OZONE

Ozone is present at low levels in the atmosphere, at close to ground level. Although ozone is a toxic gas it is considered relatively safe if it is at quantities less than 30 ppb (parts per billion). It is now quite clear that a number of human activities are responsible for increasing the amount of ozone at ground level to a level where it can be dangerous to human health.

OZONE PAPER
For the Relief and Cure of
ASTHMA,
CHRONIC BRONCHITIS. and
BRONCHITIC ASTHMA.

Low-level ozone is one of the pollutant gases that can create significant problems for people with respiratory conditions such as asthma, particularly the elderly and young children. It is not surprising to find it monitored carefully in order to provide warnings for the vulnerable groups when readings reach critical levels.

Ozone can not only damage human health but affect animals, trees, and other plants and is believed to damage rubber, nylon, plastics, dyes, and paints. The financial cost of replacing and repairing structures containing these materials can be immense.

Low-level ozone can contribute to acid rain and the enhanced greenhouse effect and is also partly responsible for photochemical smog. Ozone is a by-product of fossil fuel burning. When pollutants such as hydrocarbons and nitrogen oxides react with sunlight they produce ozone. Photochemical smog is a complex pollutant which can be generated when the reaction takes place in strong sunlight which makes the problem acute in urban areas with high sunshine levels, such as in California, and particularly during the summer months. The prevailing winds can blow the pollutants away from urban areas where they are carried across to rural areas.

Left: Ozone pollution research. Trees inside a FACE (Free-Air CO_2/O_3 Enrichment) ring for studying the effects of ozone (O_3) and carbon dioxide (CO_2) pollution on plants. O_3 and/or CO_2 are pumped into the air from the top of 8 feet tall vertical pipes (white). These trees have been damaged by ozone, which is a pollutant gas formed by chemical reactions between oxygen and pollutants in the lower atmosphere. The levels of ozone are expected to rise with increased industrialization and temperature changes. Carbon dioxide increases plant growth, but ozone reduces it.

Above: Advertisement for ozone paper from the 1880s. Inhalation of the smoke released from burning this paper was claimed to cure and relieve the symptoms of asthma and bronchitis. Ozone, a form of oxygen, is not produced when burning paper, and is poisonous to humans.

GLOBAL WARMING

It would be foolish to assume that one or two hot summers or exceptionally cold winters herald the onset of significant climate change but a significant body of evidence now exists to suggest that these freak events are part of a trend. The Intergovernmental Panel on Climate Change (IPCC), established in 1988, announced that "most of the warming observed over the last 50 years is likely to be attributable to human activities." This was the first occasion on which they had drawn the conclusion that climate change and human activity were linked.

Global temperatures have increased by 1°F in the last 150 years with most of that rise being since the 1960s. The 1990s was the warmest decade on record with 1998 being the warmest year since reliable records began in 1861. In fact four out of the five warmest years ever recorded were in the 1990s.

Sea levels have already risen globally by 4–8 inches over the last century: sea ice in the Arctic is thinning and rainfall is increasing in some parts of the world. The Greenland ice sheet is thinning at a rate of more than three feet a year in places. Recent evidence suggests that as much as 12 cubic miles of ice each year is being lost from the whole of this area. Snow cover has declined by about 10 percent in the Northern Hemisphere and mountain glaciers in non-polar regions have retreated significantly during the latter part of the 20th century. Mount Kilimanjaro in Tanzania has lost about 82 percent of the mass of its ice cap since it was first measured in 1912 and about one third from the top in the last dozen years. Peru's Quelccaya ice sheet in the Southern Andes has lost 20 percent of its mass since 1963. In the mid and high latitude parts of the Northern Hemisphere there has been a two to four percent increase in the frequency of heavy rainfall, and the frequency and intensity of drought in Asia and Africa has increased in the last few decades. How much of this really proves that major global climate change is taking place remains to be seen.

Aerial view of the edge of the Greenland ice sheet. The extent of the sheet is determined by the seasons, but a large amount of the most northern areas is always covered.

GLOBAL DIMMING

In 2001 a report was published by Gerry Stanhill, a British scientist, in which he showed that the amount of sunlight reaching the Earth had fallen. Stanhill was working in Israel and had compared sunshine records there from the 1950s with those of the present day and discovered that there had been a 22 percent drop in the amount of sunlight received. He went on to study the sunlight records from around the world and discovered falls of 10 percent in the USA, almost 30 percent in parts of the former Soviet Union and 16 percent in parts of the British Isles. The amount of sunshine reduction varied from place to place, but the global average per decade between the 1950s and 1990s was between one and two percent. He described the phenomenon as global dimming. Although his results were greeted with some scepticism by other scientists, his conclusions were recently confirmed by scientists in Australia who had used a completely different method.

Global dimming seems to be caused by the burning of fossil fuels which produces carbon dioxide but also particles of soot, ash, and sulfur compounds; in other words, atmospheric pollution appears to be the cause. Particles in the atmosphere reflect some sunlight back into space and also change the optical properties of clouds. The particles act as hygroscopic nuclei, the particles around which water molecules collect, and so clouds in polluted areas will contain more water droplets than those in non-polluted areas. According to recent research this makes clouds reflect more of the sun's rays back into space.

There are now suggestions that dimming was responsible for the droughts of sub-Saharan Africa of the 1970s and 1980s. By reducing the amount of sunshine that reaches the oceans, dimming may be disrupting the world's rainfall patterns. The drought in Africa claimed thousands of lives; any future disruption of rainfall could be equally catastrophic.

A thick smog, containing dust and soot particles, darkens a busy street in the city of Buenos Aires, Argentina. It is thought that atmospheric pollution is the cause of global dimming.

DESERTIFICATION

The world's great deserts, such as the Sahara, have developed naturally over many hundreds and thousands of years. They have advanced or retreated entirely independently of human activity during this time. There is now some evidence to suggest that the rate of spread of desert areas has increased and that this may be in part due to human activity and global climate change.

Where a desert begins and ends is often difficult to determine and the transitional zone is sometimes gradual. Human activity in these transitional zones may be critical to the formation or extension of deserts. Where human population has increased there may be intolerable pressures on the fragile ecosystems of arid and semi-arid desert-transitional zones. Overgrazing of animals, the cutting down of trees for firewood and poor agricultural techniques may be responsible for degradation of the soil and its ability to support vegetation. Topsoil may turn to dust and be blown away. One prediction for the latter half of the 21st century is that the East African countries of Kenya, Mozambique, and Tanzania will experience slightly warmer weather but will be challenged by persistent drought. The inevitable consequences will be a real threat to the food supply from the grain-producing parts of the region. Warmer temperatures will also increase the rate of evaporation in areas already vulnerable, exacerbating the problems people there will have to face in the future. Northern and western Europe are predicted to experience increased soil erosion as rainfall reduces, and the soil dries and is blown away by increasingly strong winds. This currently productive area will be likely to suffer food shortages as a result. Much of the developed world is not self-sufficient in food production but can afford to import; however, any further reductions will lead to significantly increased problems for the area in future. The unusual droughts there in 1976 and 2006 have hinted at the problems that may become more common as global warming develops.

Skeletal remains in Sossusvlei, Namibia. Sand dunes are formed from windblown sand. The sand accumulates into ridges or furrows that originally lie parallel to the direction of the prevailing winds. Ripples form as sand is transported and deposited by wind. There are three main types of desert: sandy deserts or ergs, rocky deserts or hammada, and stony deserts or reg. Deserts are made in different ways, but they are always formed because there is not enough water. Only about 25 percent of the world's deserts are sandy.

EL NIÑO

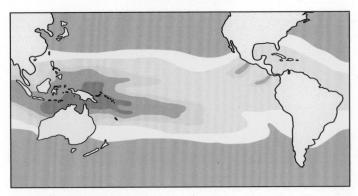

La Niña January - March 1989

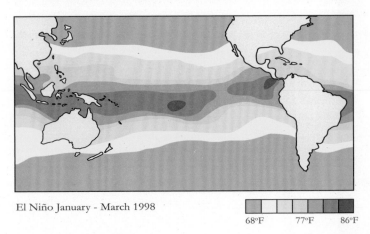

El Niño January - March 1998

68°F   77°F   86°F

In September 2006 a report stated that sea surface temperatures in the eastern Pacific had risen by 1.5°C in less than two weeks. This, it appeared, was the beginning of an El Niño event. Droughts, floods, and increased hurricane activity are all associated with El Niño and with its counterpart in the equatorial Pacific, La Niña.

An El Niño event is a disruption of the ocean-atmosphere system in the tropical Pacific. It brings warm water to the eastern Pacific and is associated with unusual weather across the globe. The phenomenon was initially recognized by fishermen off the Pacific coast of South America who identified unusually warm water at the start of the year. El Niño is a Spanish term meaning little boy or Christ Child as the weather phenomenon tends to develop around the Christmas period. It is thought to recur every 11 years or so but can develop more frequently: in 1986–87; 1991–92 and again in 1997–98.

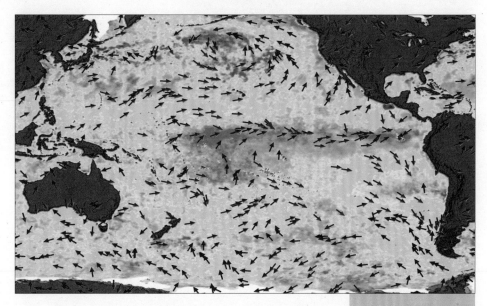

Normally the trade winds blow towards the west across the tropical parts of the Pacific. Warm surface water piles up in the western Pacific driven by the trade winds which means that the sea may be two feet higher near Indonesia compared with its level off the Ecuador coast. Sea surface temperatures are about 8°C higher in the west than in the cool-water areas of the east, where cold water from the depths rises to the surface bringing with it many nutrients. These cool seas are responsible for the marine diversity of the region. In this easterly area there is relatively little rainfall, but there is considerably more in the west as air warmed by the sea rises and is blown the westwards across the land.

The situation is different in an El Niño year, however, and the trade winds relax in the central and western Pacific. Sea surface temperatures rise in the eastern Pacific and with this comes the increased rainfall normally associated with lands further west. This can bring flooding to the western parts of South America such as Peru and conversely less rainfall over the west in countries like Australia and Indonesia, perhaps even drought. The changes are not confined to the Pacific as El Niño is recognized as having an impact on global circulation and an impact on weather around the world.

Above: Satellite data from the 2002–03 El Niño shows anomalies in sea surface temperature (SST) and the direction of the wind in the Pacific Ocean. The SST data shows areas that are hotter (orange) and cooler (blue) than normal. Wind direction is shown by the arrows.

Opposite: Normally trade winds blow west and the sea may be 14°F warmer in the west than in the east (top), where deep, cold water rises to the surface. In an El Niño year the trade winds relax and sea surface temperatures rise in the eastern Pacific.

SEA LEVEL RISE

One of the most worrying potential effects of global warming, natural or anthropogenic, is the predicted rise in sea level. Already a number of low-lying island nations such as Tuvalu have experienced problems with flooding but the pattern is predicted to continue and to become more widespread.

In a report published in early 2006, Australian researchers led by Dr John Church found that sea levels had risen by 8 inches between 1870 and 2004 with most of that occuring during the last 50 years. The Commonwealth Scientific and Industrial Research Organization used tide gauges from around the world to prepare the information on which their conclusions were based. They went on to predict future sea level rises of up to 13 inches during the 21st century if current trends continue. The international organization the Intergovernmental Panel on Climate Change (IPCC) predicted broadly the same conclusions, although a worst-case scenario indicated a possible 34 inch increase during that time.

The cause of the projected increase is the warming of the Earth's atmosphere which will lead to a number of events. One of these is the melting of mountain glaciers and ice sheets such as the Greenland ice sheet. Thermal expansion of the sea water is also predicted and would be a future cause of sea level rise. The West Antarctic ice sheet is of some concern to scientists at present. They estimate that if it melted the sea level could rise by 20 feet. It is generally believed the sea level was 20 feet higher than today during the last inter-glacial period, the time when virtually no permanent ice existed on the Earth's surface.

A complete melting of the Greenland ice sheet would, it is believed, cause a 23 feet rise in sea levels but even a partial melt could see a rise of three feet. A rise of this magnitude would entirely submerge the Maldive Islands and devastate countries like Bangladesh, 50 percent of which lies less than 16 feet above sea level.

Icebergs from the Roseg glacier in a lake in the Roseg valley in the Swiss Alps. The valley used to be covered in ice from the Roseg and Tschierva glaciers. Warming of the climate has led to these glaciers retreating in the last few decades. A moraine (pile of rocky debris) left by the retreat of the Tschierva glacier has blocked the valley and led to the formation of this lake.

THE GULF STREAM

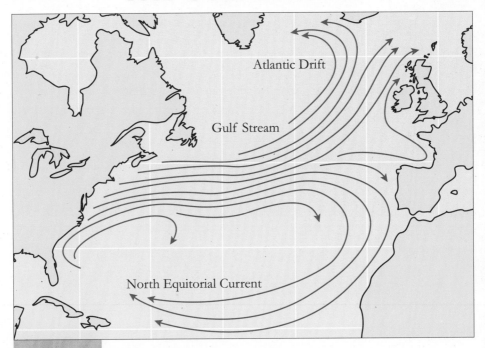

Atlantic Drift

Gulf Stream

North Equitorial Current

Map showing the course of the Gulf Stream, the strongest ocean current in the northern hemisphere. An interruption of the current might have devestating consequences on the global climate.

The Hollywood blockbuster *The Day After Tomorrow*, released in 2004, brought the attention of a wider audience to one importance of the Gulf Stream in determining the weather in the Northern Hemisphere. The movie centers on a meteorologist who predicts that the Gulf Stream will shortly shut down and bring a series of catastrophic weather events that will precipitate a new Ice Age.

So, what is the Gulf Stream? It is the strongest ocean current in the Northern Hemisphere which carries about 30 billion gallons of water per second. It is a branch of the global thermohaline circulation (THC) that is driven by differences in temperature and salinity. It brings warm water north from the Caribbean to the UK and the rest of north-west Europe. It is responsible for the latter region's temperate climate. Despite being at broadly the same latitude as Newfoundland in north-eastern Canada the UK never suffers from the extreme cold that causes the sea to freeze. The Gulf Stream is responsible for the longer growing season of the coastal parts of western Europe—it is possible to grow semi-tropical plants as far north as Scotland due to the warming effect of the current.

If, however, global temperatures continue to rise then, it is feared, the Greenland Ice Cap will melt. Rainfall will replace snowfall at high latitudes causing potential disruption as it will increase the freshwater and decrease the salinity content of the North Atlantic. This could lead to the complete shut-down of the North Atlantic circulation. If the Gulf Stream shuts down then north-west Europe will become very much colder. This would take a lot longer than the movie suggests, but recent research published in 2006 has suggested it may take as little as a few decades. The UK could see temperatures fall by as much as 5° or 7°F which would mean very much colder winters according to the Hadley Center, a meteorological research institute. The difference in temperatures between the "Little Ice Age" of the 16th and 17th centuries and the medieval warm period was only 1 or 2 degrees so 3 or 4 degrees is quite significant. The Hadley Center also says that summers would become shorter and cooler, creating a shorter growing season, and so the implications for agriculture are immense. Ice core samples from the Polar regions show regular climate changes have occurred in the past with temperature fluctuations of perhaps as much as 9–18°F in as short a time as a decade. Recent research implicates oceanic circulation in many of these changes.

Water flow in the Gulf Stream seen from the shuttle Endeavour. This view, looking roughly south-west, shows the boundary between water in the Gulf Stream and the coastal waters off the eastern USA. Sunglint highlights the difference between the two—the warmer, fast flowing Gulf Stream (lower half) shows complex eddies whereas the coastal waters are calmer.

INCREASED STORMS

The summer hurricane season of 2005 was particularly famous for the effects of Hurricane Katrina which devastated New Orleans and much of the Gulf of Texas in the USA. Inevitably, this and the other powerful hurricanes of that season fed the rumor mill with many suggesting that this was the precursor to a marked increase in the effects of global warming. According to a 2004 report from the Georgia Institute of Technology the 15-year period 1975–89 experienced 171 severe hurricanes, that is those of category 4 or 5 on the Saffir-Simpson scale. They reported that the figure rose to 269 in the period from 1990 to 2004. The reason for this, they argued, was that the sea surface temperature had increased, a particular manifestation of global warming, and was now about 2°F above the long-term average.

Using 22 computer models of different climate scenarios they deduced that there was an 84 percent chance that human activity was responsible for at least 66 percent of sea surface temperature increase in the Pacific Typhoon and Atlantic Hurricane areas. Hurricane formation over the Atlantic appears to occur in phases which change every few decades. The 1940s and 1950s were active; the 1970s and 1980s were not. The current, more active phase appears to have started in about 1995. It is also worth remembering that not all hurricanes hit land and so not all are reported as thoroughly as was Katrina.

In Europe, there was the Great Storm of 1987 over northern France and southern England, and the floods that affected much of Europe in the summer of 2002 with the flooding of Vienna, Austria being the worst for a century: numerous reports worldwide of local, damaging floods such as these caused by unusual storms have emerged. These events are widely reported in part because they reflect increasing concern about the frequency and severity of storms, other than those of hurricane force, and their likely association with global warming. It is these that may affect more and more people as time passes; more people now live on flood plains than ever before and so it is inevitable that even small floods will have a greater impact on homes and property.

Torrential rain, which may accompany a hurricane or other violent storm, often causes flooding and triggers landslides and mudslides. These may then sweep away highways, bridges, railroads and sometimes even whole towns.

HEATWAVES

Global map showing the increased temperatures compared to previous years, during the heatwave in the Northern Hemisphere in the summer of 2006. The average land surface temperature from 12–19 July 2006 was compared to the average temperature during the same period averaged over the previous six years (2000–2005). Red indicates hotter temperatures and blue indicates cooler temperatures.

A total of 740 deaths in Chicago, USA, in the summer of 1995 and almost 15,000 deaths in France in the summer of 2003 were attributed to heat waves of unusual intensity. These are figures which seem alarming but which many climate scientists believe we should come to expect if predicitons of increased frequency of such heat waves because of global warming are to be believed.

The United States Center for Atmospheric Research (NCAR) used climate modeling techniques to predict the geography of future heat waves and concluded that Europe and North America were most likely to experience more frequent, longer, and more intense heat waves. These were predicted to coincide with an atmospheric circulation intensified by an increase in the amount of greenhouse gases present.

Particularly severe heat waves were predicted to occur in a belt stretching from the Mediterranean Sea and western USA northward. The Balkans, France, and Germany may be increasingly susceptible to heat waves such as those of 2003. The city of Chicago was predicted to experience a 25 percent increase in such events whereas Paris would experience up to 31 percent more, posing problems for the city authorities as they prepare for the future.

DISEASE

Global warming is predicted to have a significant impact on the future global distribution of diseases. Those currently found only in the Tropics may in future be common in higher latitudes if predicted temperature rises take place.

One disease for which there is currently no preventive vaccine and which affects some 600 million people worldwide is malaria. The malarial mosquito is the Anopheles gambiae variety found in the Tropics and the disease is carried by the female alone. The mosquito lays its eggs on a stagnant water surface from which the larvae hatch. These will be carriers of the parasite and can go on to spread the disease further. If warming does take place in higher latitudes then it may be possible for the disease to spread to countries such as those in Europe which currently are malaria-free. Already malaria has been detected in new and higher-elevation areas in Indonesia. Mosquitoes that can carry dengue fever viruses were previously limited to land up to 3300 feet but recently appeared at 7200 feet in the Andes Mountains of Colombia. The cost to those countries' economies will be immense, to say nothing of the impact on human health.

Global warming might affect the distribution of disease. If temperatures rise then tropical diseases, such as malaria, might become more common at higher latitudes. Mosquitoes carrying other diseases are already spreading as climate shifts allow them to survive in formerly inhospitable areas.

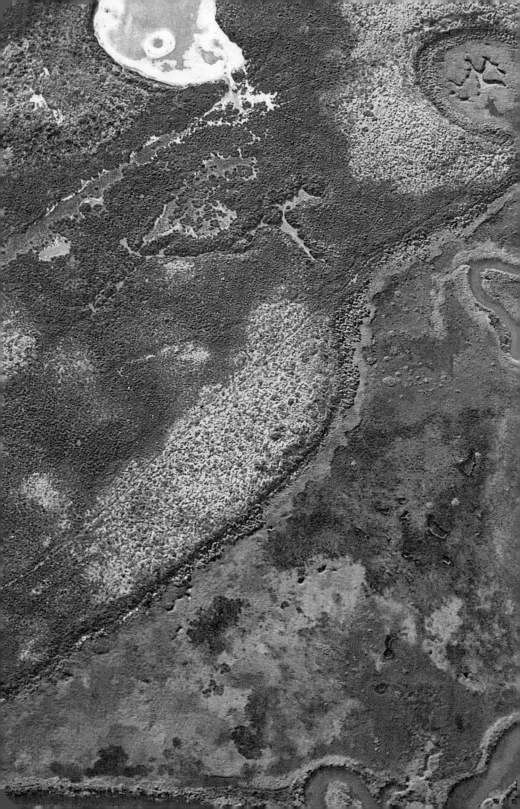

POPULATION MIGRATION

With over 400 million people living in drier, sub-tropical, often over-populated and economically poor regions today, climate change and its associated effects pose a severe risk to the political, economic, and social stability of many nations. In poor countries where there is a lack of resources and capabilities to adapt quickly to more severe conditions, the problem is very likely to be exacerbated. For some, mass emigration may be the result as desperate people look for a better life in regions such as the USA that have the resources to adapt. One such country is Bangladesh; one prediction for the country by the mid-21st century is for persistent typhoons and higher sea level storm surges which will cause significant coastal erosion and make much of the country uninhabitable. As sea levels rise there will be contamination of fresh drinking water supplies leading to a humanitarian crisis that is predicted to lead to mass emigration. Tension between Bangladesh and China and India, all of which may struggle to cope, will increase as the migrants head for those countries.

It has been suggested that the continent to be hardest hit by climate change, however, is Europe. A temperature fall of 6°F in less than a decade has been predicted. Even more dramatic falls along the north-western coasts are predicted making the area drier, windier, and much more like Siberia. Mass emigration from Scandinavia and other northern European countries may take place as people search for a warmer climate. Southern Europe may be squeezed by both the emigrating northern Europeans and those leaving the hard-hit parts of Africa. Emigration from the latter continent has already been a common feature—and controversial issue—in Europe for many decades. How well the continent will be able to cope is difficult to predict but it is unlikely to be easy.

Higher sea levels and storm surges are a threat to populations living on coastal plains.

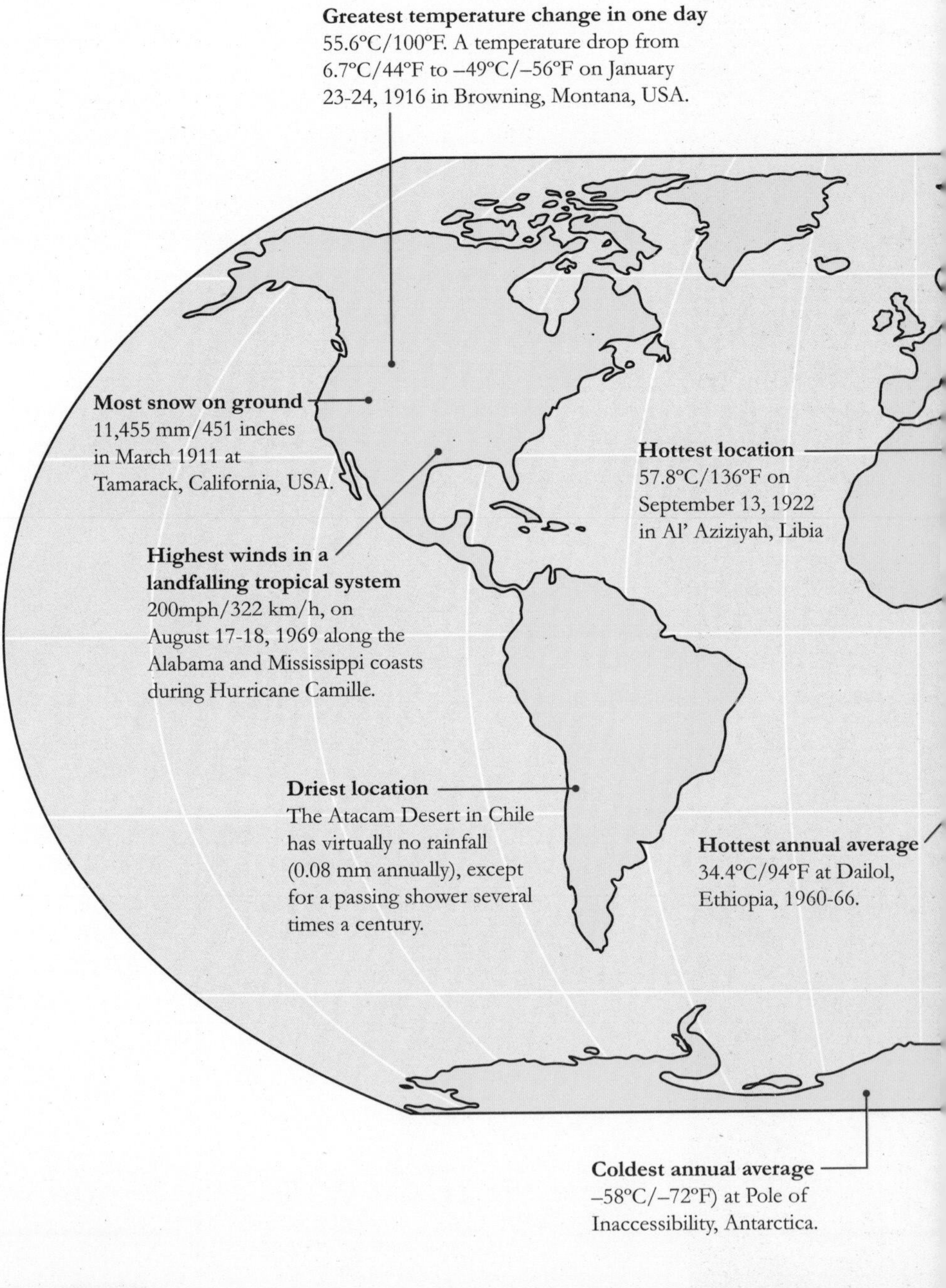

Greatest temperature change in one day
55.6°C/100°F. A temperature drop from
6.7°C/44°F to –49°C/–56°F on January
23-24, 1916 in Browning, Montana, USA.

Most snow on ground
11,455 mm/451 inches
in March 1911 at
Tamarack, California, USA.

Hottest location
57.8°C/136°F on
September 13, 1922
in Al' Aziziyah, Libia

**Highest winds in a
landfalling tropical system**
200mph/322 km/h, on
August 17-18, 1969 along the
Alabama and Mississippi coasts
during Hurricane Camille.

Driest location
The Atacam Desert in Chile
has virtually no rainfall
(0.08 mm annually), except
for a passing shower several
times a century.

Hottest annual average
34.4°C/94°F at Dailol,
Ethiopia, 1960-66.

Coldest annual average
–58°C/–72°F) at Pole of
Inaccessibility, Antarctica.

WEATHER RECORDS

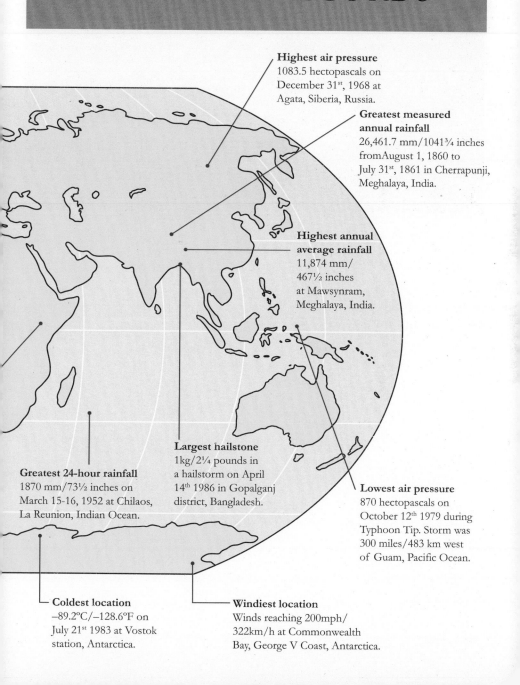

Highest air pressure
1083.5 hectopascals on
December 31st, 1968 at
Agata, Siberia, Russia.

**Greatest measured
annual rainfall**
26,461.7 mm/1041¾ inches
fromAugust 1, 1860 to
July 31st, 1861 in Cherrapunji,
Meghalaya, India.

**Highest annual
average rainfall**
11,874 mm/
467½ inches
at Mawsynram,
Meghalaya, India.

Largest hailstone
1kg/2¼ pounds in
a hailstorm on April
14th 1986 in Gopalganj
district, Bangladesh.

Lowest air pressure
870 hectopascals on
October 12th 1979 during
Typhoon Tip. Storm was
300 miles/483 km west
of Guam, Pacific Ocean.

Greatest 24-hour rainfall
1870 mm/73½ inches on
March 15-16, 1952 at Chilaos,
La Reunion, Indian Ocean.

Coldest location
−89.2°C/−128.6°F on
July 21st 1983 at Vostok
station, Antarctica.

Windiest location
Winds reaching 200mph/
322km/h at Commonwealth
Bay, George V Coast, Antarctica.

TEMPERATURE

HIGHEST

The highest temperatures ever recorded by continent:

Africa: El Azizia in Libya at an elevation of 367 feet experienced the world's highest temperature of 136°F on September 13, 1922.

North America: The Greenland Ranch in Death Valley, California, USA, is 78 feet below sea level and it experienced a temperature which reached 134°F on July 10, 1913.

Asia: The highest temperature recorded here occurred in Israel at Tirat Tsvi on June 22, 1942. Like Death Valley this area too is below sea level, some 722 feet. The temperature experienced here was 129°F.

Australia: Cloncurry, Queensland, is at 622 feet above sea level. It experienced a temperature of 128°F on January 16, 1889. Given the date there maybe some doubt as to the validity of this figure as the instruments available then were different from the standard used today.

Europe: August 4, 1881 saw the hottest ever temperature recorded in Europe in Seville, southern Spain. Here a temperature of 122°F was recorded in this Andalusian city.

South America: In 1905, Rivadavia in Argentina recorded 120°F, the hottest ever in South America.

Oceania: On April 29, 1912, a record 108°F was recorded at Tuguegarao in the Philippines.

LOWEST

The lowest temperatures ever recorded by continent.

The world's highest temperature was recorded at Al Azizayah, in the Libyan Sahara on September 13, 1922.

Asia: The honor of second place is shared by two stations in Asian Russia – Siberia. The settlements of Oimekon and Verkhoyansk both experienced –90°F), the former on February 6, 1933 whereas the latter was on February 7, 1892.

North America: The Yukon, Canada is the location of the continent's lowest temperature of –81.4°F on February 3, 1847.

Europe: On a January day (the precise date is unknown) European Russia experience its, and the continent's, lowest temperature of –67°F at Ust'Shchugor.

South America: Argentina's and the continent's lowest temperature of –27°F occurred at Sarmiento on January 1, 1907.

Africa: At an elevation of 5364 feet, Ifrane in Morocco experienced a temperature of –11°F on February 11, 1935.

Australia: Australia is not a part of the world normally associated with very cold temperatures but Charlotte Pass, New South Wales, at an elevation of 5758 feet experienced –9.4°F on June 29, 1994.

Oceania: In May 1979 at an elevation of 13,773 feet, the Mauna Kea Observatory on Hawaii experienced the continent's lowest temperature, 12°F.

PRECIPITATION

WETTEST PLACE (annual averages)

South America: 523.6 inches of rain falls on average each year in Lloro, Colombia.

Asia: This continent's highest total is believed to be Mawsynram, India. Its high elevation, 4597 feet, may have helped it to reach its total average of 467.4 inches each year.

Oceania: Hawaii, once again, holds this record with Mount Waialeale receiving 460 inches each year.

Africa: The country of Cameroon holds his continent's record. At Debundscha 405 inches of rain is the annual average total.

Australia: At an altitude of 5102 feet above sea level, Bellenden Ker in tropical Queensland holds Australia's record. A hefty average of 340 inches of rainfall occurs here each year.

North America: British Columbia in Canada holds North America's record. At Henderson Lake the annual average is 256 inches.

Europe: At Crkvica in Bosnia Herzegovina, at an altitude of 3337 feet, the annual average is 183 inches. This record has been held for 22 years.

DRIEST PLACE (annual averages)

South America: This occurs in the Atacama Desert in Chile. Between 1964 and 2001 the annual average rainfall total at Quillaga was less than 0.2 inches. At Arica, also in Chile, there is annually an average of three thousandths of an inch.

The worst death toll from a lightning strike occurred when a Boeing 707–121 jet liner was struck by lightning near Elkton, Maryland, USA on December 8, 1963. Eighty-one people were killed when the lightning strike ignited fuel vapor causing a mid-air explosion.

Africa: At Wadi Halfa, Sudan, less than 0.1 inches of rain falls annually, a record that has stood for almost 40 years.

North America: Mexico holds this record; at Batagues only 1.2 inches of rain falls on average every year.

Asia: Aden, Yemen, holds Africa's record for the lowest annual average rainfall. At just 1.8 inches, the record has been held for 50 years.

Australia: Mulka, South Australia holds this continent's record of 4.05 inches.

Europe: The city of Astrakhan in Russia experiences only 6.4 inches of rain every year.

Oceania: 8.93 inches of rain is the expected annual average on this continent. The record is held by Puako, Hawaii.

SUN AND RAIN

Greatest number of consecutive sunny days: Between February 9, 1967 and March 17, 1969 St Petersburg in Florida, experienced 768 consecutive days of sunshine.

Greatest hours of sunshine: Sunny Yuma, Arizona receives an average of 4055 of 4456 possible hours of sunshine each year, 91 percent of the total possible.

Most rainy days: At 5144 feet above sea level, Kauai in Hawaii was always likely to experience a great deal of rain but there are usually only two days when it doesn't rain. On average this area receives up to 350 rainy days each year and these bring almost 500 inches of rain each year.

Most thunder days per year: Tororo, Uganda, holds the world record of an average of 251 days of thunder each year, based on calculations taken between 1967 and 1976.

WIND

Windiest place at high altitude
The USA holds this record on Mount Washington in New Hampshire at an altitude of 6288 feet. On March 12, 1934 the wind speed reached 231 miles per hour.

Windiest place at low altitude
The fastest surface wind speed found at low altitude occurred in Thule, Greenland on March 8, 1972. At the local USAF base they recorded 207 miles per hour.

Tornadoes – the greatest number per area
Although most people would assume that the United States would have most reported tornadoes in this category this is not the case. Instead, that honor falls to the UK. In the USA there is one reported tornado per 2856 square miles. In the UK, however, the reported number is one per 2856 square miles.

Tornadoes – the greatest number in 24 hours
Not surprisingly this record is held by the infamous Tornado Alley area of the USA. Here, on April 3 and 4, 1974 a staggering 148 tornadoes were recorded.

Tornadoes – the largest
Once again, Tornado Alley in the USA holds this record. Mulhall in north Oklahoma experienced a huge tornado onMay 2, 1999. This, one of 70 which occurred that day, was 5250 feet in diameter and caused 40 deaths.

SNOWFALL AND HAILSTONES

Pedestrians battle against snow and wind. The most snow to fall on the ground was recorded on March 11, 1911, when 451 inches fell in Tamarack, California.

Highest Annual Amount of Snowfall:
The volcano Mount Rainier holds this record. Between February 1971 and February 1972 4224 inches of snow fell.

Highest Amount of Snowfall in One Day:
The world record for the greatest amount of snow fall on one day was an astonishing 76 inches at Silver Lake, Colorado, USA on April 15, 1921.

In Canada the highest amount fell on February 11, 1999 in Tahtsa Lake, British Columbia, Canada. Here 57 inches fell in a single day.

Highest Amount of Snow from a Single Snowstorm:
Another American volcano holds this record.
In 1959, during a storm which occurred between
February 13 and 19, at Ski Bowl on Mount Shasta,
189 inches of snow fell.

Largest Snowflake:
According to records from January 1887 an
enormous snowflake fell on Fort Keogh in
Montana, USA. This flake was reported to have
been 15 inches in diameter and 8 inches thick. This
one alone would have made several very useful
snowballs!

Heaviest Hailstone:
The world's heaviest hailstone fell in Bangladesh
in April 1986. This weighed 2.25 pounds and fell in
a storm which killed 92 people. In 1888 in
Moradabad cricket or baseball-sized hailstones fell
killing dozens of people and up to 1600 cattle.

A large hailstone. However, the
biggest hailstone in American
history landed in Aurora,
Nebraska during a violent
thunderstorm on June 22,
2003. The piece of ice was
almost 7 inches in diameter
with a circumference of 19
inches. Hailstones grow larger
as they circulate until they are
either too heavy to be
supported by the cloud or are
thrown out of the updraft area.

INDEX

ACKNOWLEDGMENTS

Science Photo Library

Doug Allan 61; Jim Amos 200; John Beatty 98; Ben Nevis Observatory 187; Bettmann 76/77; Adrian Bicker 10/11; Martin Bond 190, 194/195, 196/197; Brian Brake 128/129; British Antarctic Survey 206, 207; Chris Butler 202; Cape Grim B.A.P.S 179; Colin Cuthbert 58b; Michael Donne 166185; Bernhard Edmaier 224/225; European Space Agency 25; Eye of Science 78; Simon Fraser 87, 186, 201; David R Frazier 93; Gordon Garradd 45; Geoeye 37; Geospace 28; Mark E Gibson 70/71; Michael Gilbert 218, 220; Pascal Goergheluck 97; Goldin Carlos 226/227; Hay Jones David 65, 172, 173, 178, 222; Kaprielian John 216/217; Paulo Koch 47; Damian Lovegrove 152/153; Magrath/Folsom 66; Marine Biological Survey 208; Jerry Mason 221; John Mead 188/189, 192/193; Peter Menzel 138, 181; G Antonio Milani 95; Carlos Munus-Yague /Meteo France/Eurelios 184; NASA 303, 440/41, 52, 67, 84, 96, 132, 139, 169, 231, 235, 238; NASA/Goddard Space Centre 117; NCAR 81; Thomas Nilsen 212/213, 214/215; NOAA 131, 182; Ria Novosti 136, 191/193; NRSC Ltd 72; David Nunuk 142/143; Sam Ogden 174, 177; David Parker 175, 183; Gary Parker 94; Pekka Parviainen 56/57, 58t, 59, 60, 63, 148/149, 150/151; George Post 127; Paul Rapson 176; Jim Reed 68, 80, 170/171, 180; Dave Reede 156; Rev. Ronald Royer 74/75b; Chris Sattlberger 116; Karsten Schneider 85; Mark A Schneider 22/23, 154/155; Science Photo Library 36, 42, 165, 167, 204/205, 223; Stammers/Sinclair 210/211; Michael Szoenyi 209, 232/233; Sheila Terry 159; Mike Theiss/Jim Reed Photography 114; Geoff Tompkinson 92; Mike Umsscheid 53; University of Dundee 38, 43; Detlev Van Ravenswaay 168; Jeremy Walker 203; Art Wolfe 64;

Digital Vision

1, 2, 3, 4, 8/9, 12, 14, 15, 16, 18, 19, 20, 24, 26, 32, 35, 39, 44 48, 51, 62, 69, 79, 82, 83, 90, 99, 100, 103, 106, 107, 108, 109, 110, 111, 112/113, 115, 118/119, 120, 121, 122, 126, 133, 140/141, 145, 146/147, 198/199, 228/229, 236/237, 240/241, 245, 246, 247, 248, 250

Getty Images

74/75t, 102, 123, 124/125, 162/163, 164, 239, 249

Corbis

17, 21, 91, 101, 104/105, 130, 134/135, 157, 158, 244, 251